This book is belongs to

Hello Winter

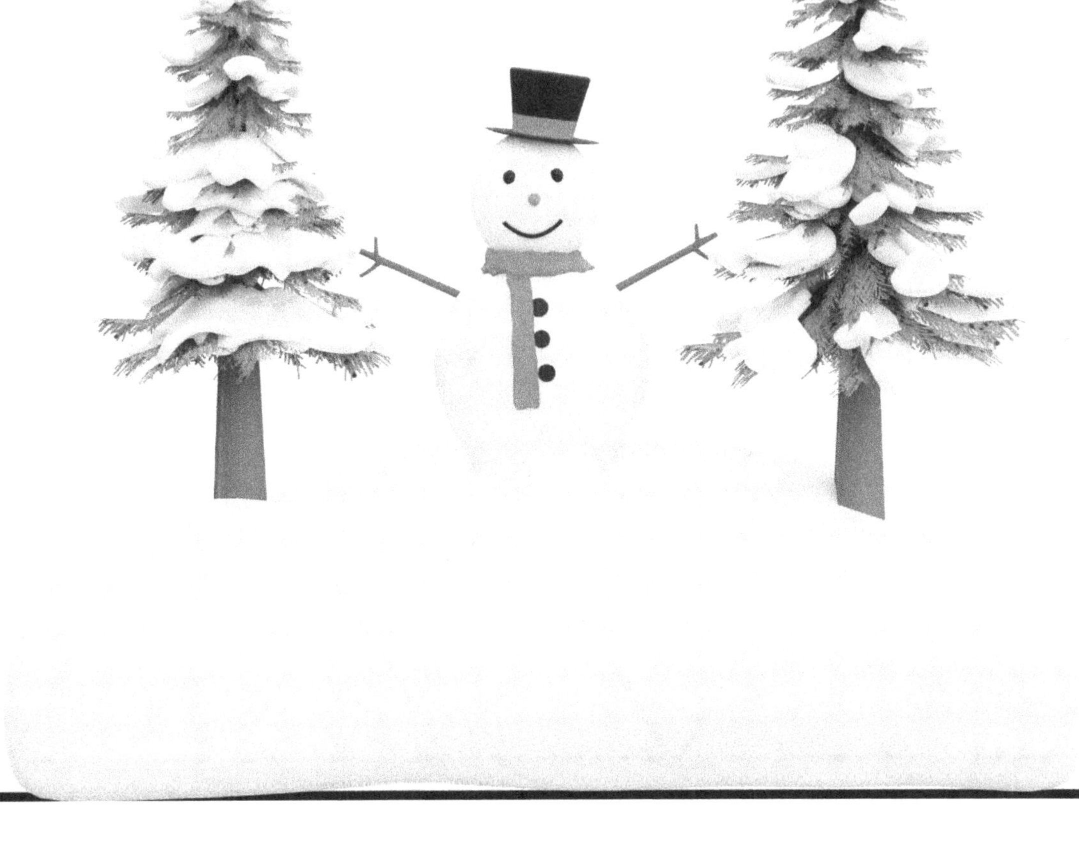

color test page

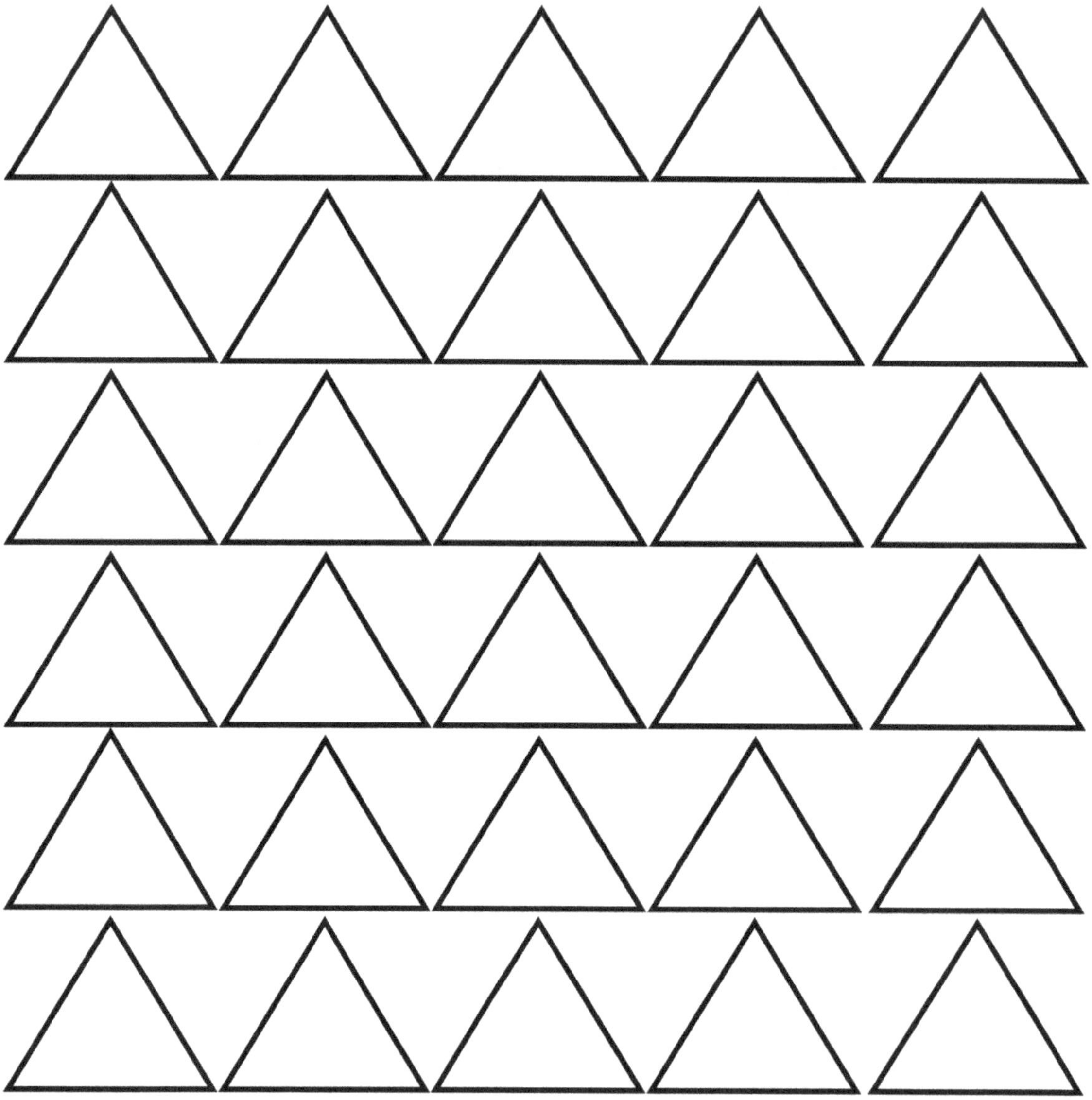

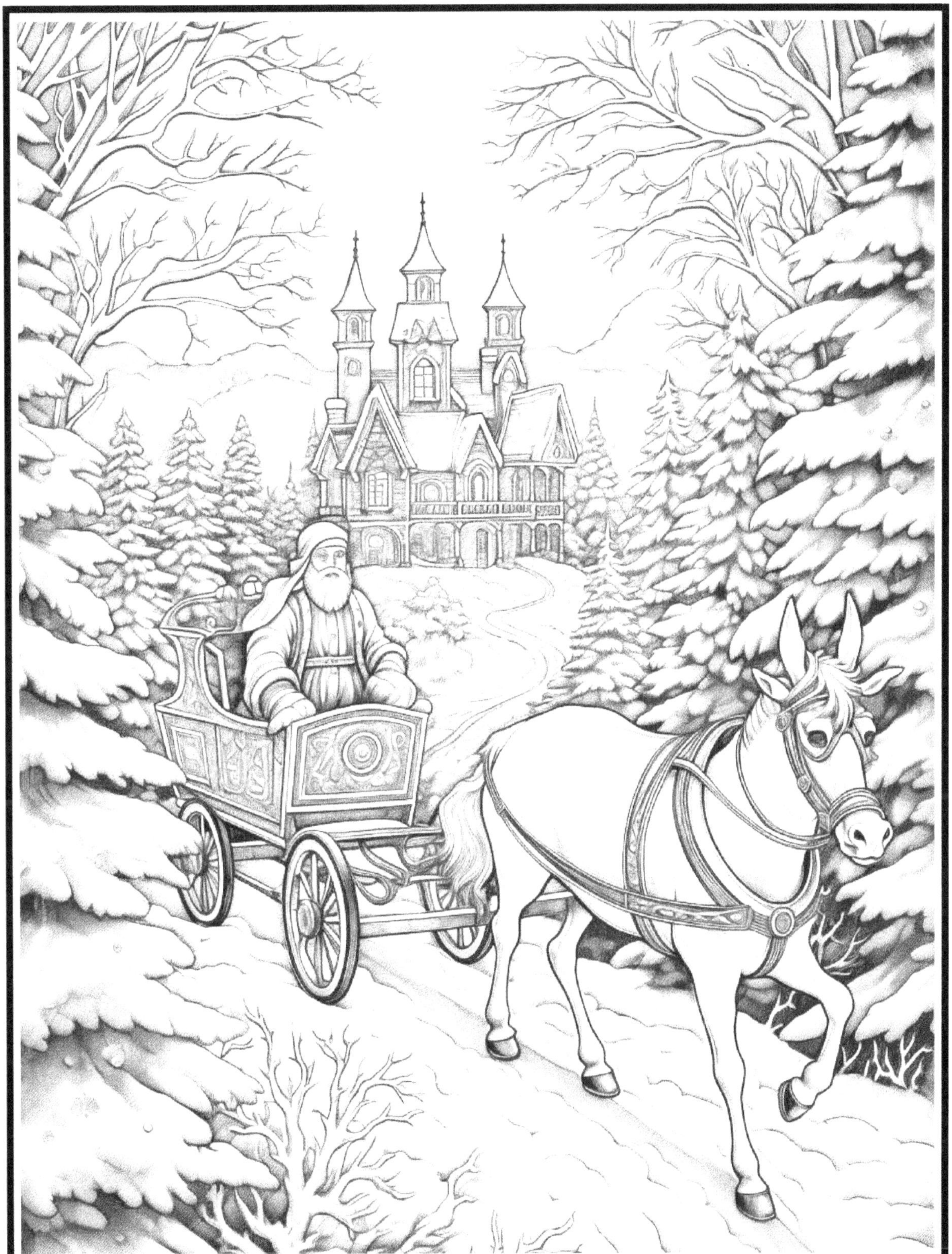

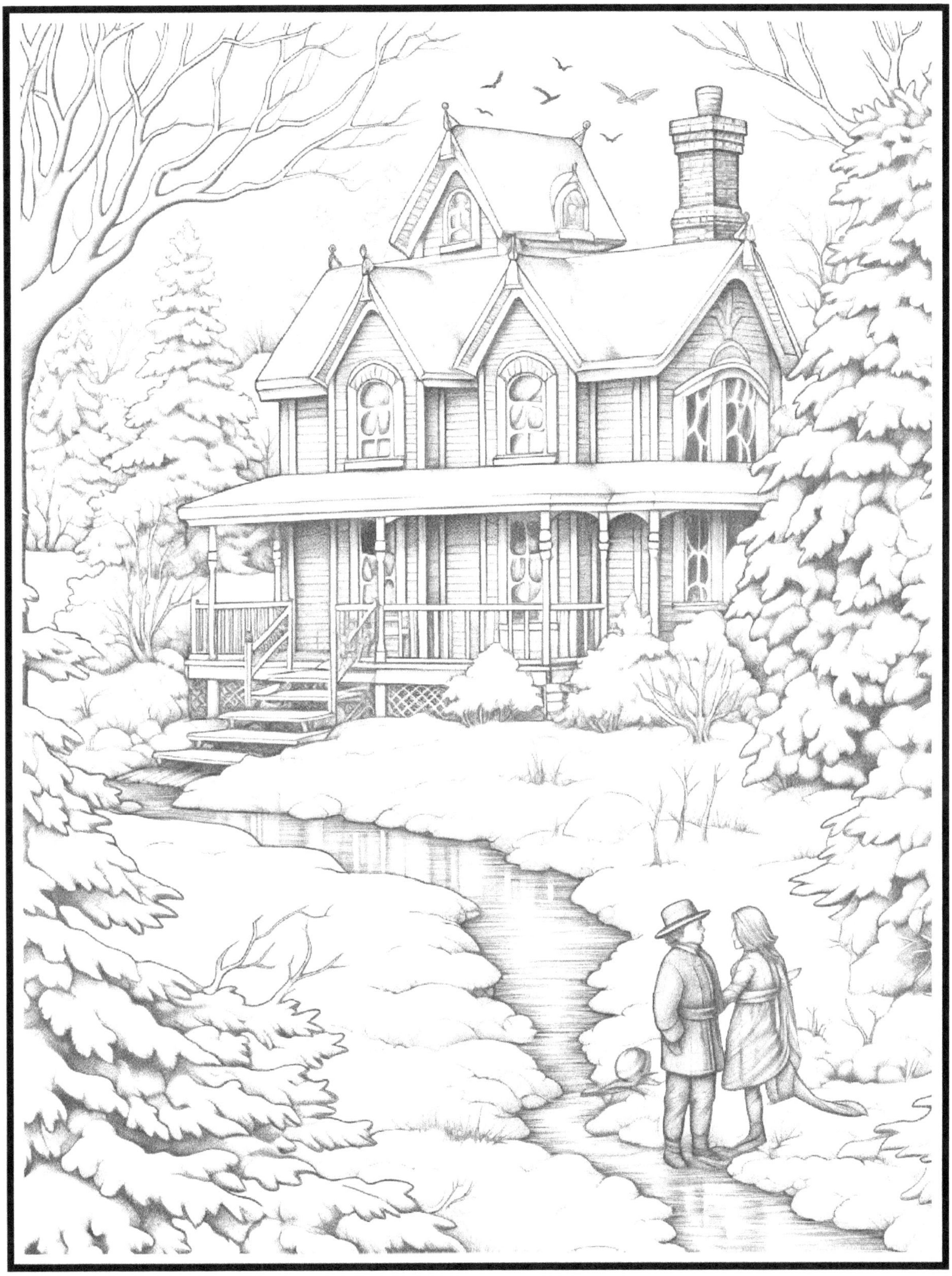

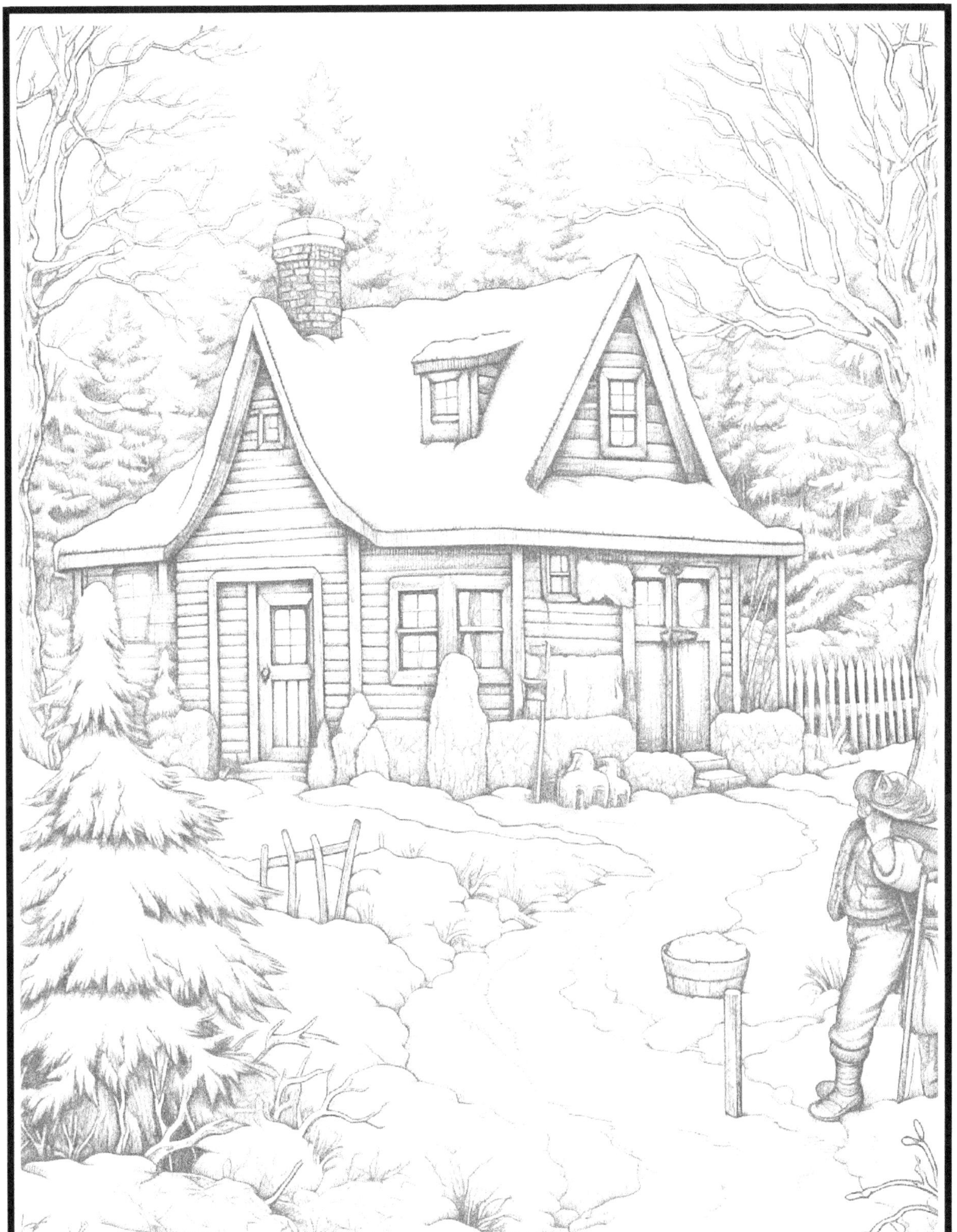

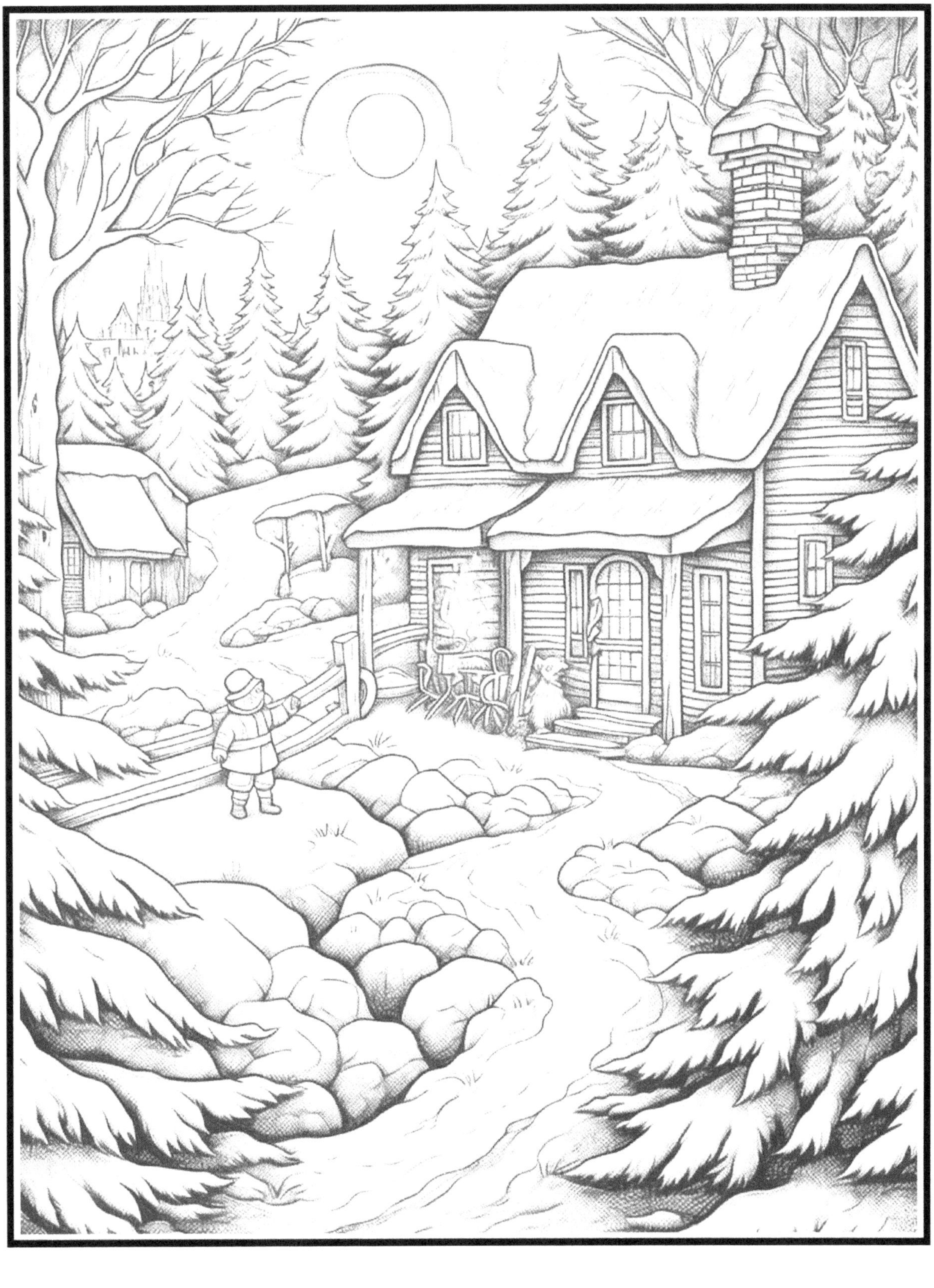

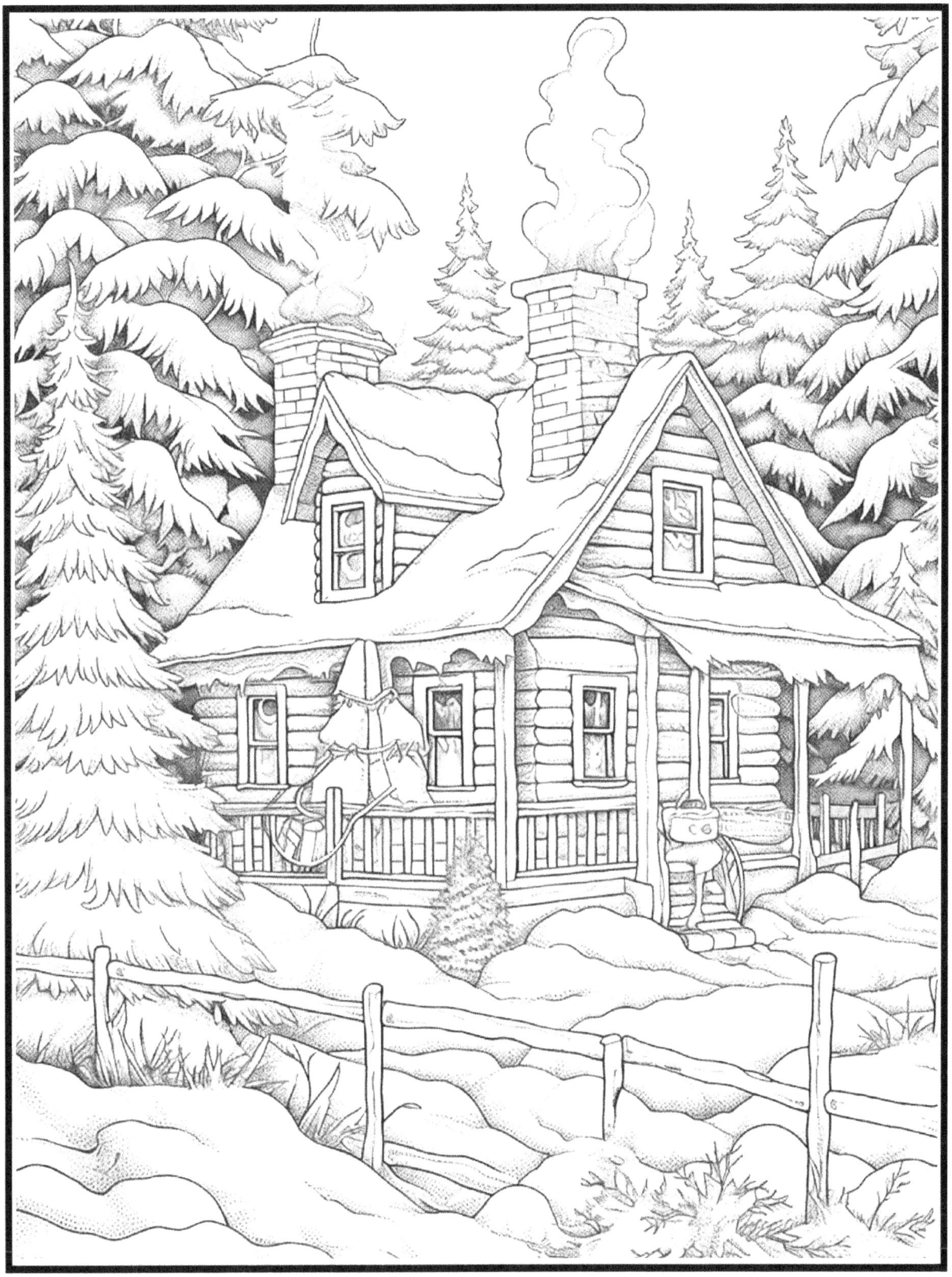

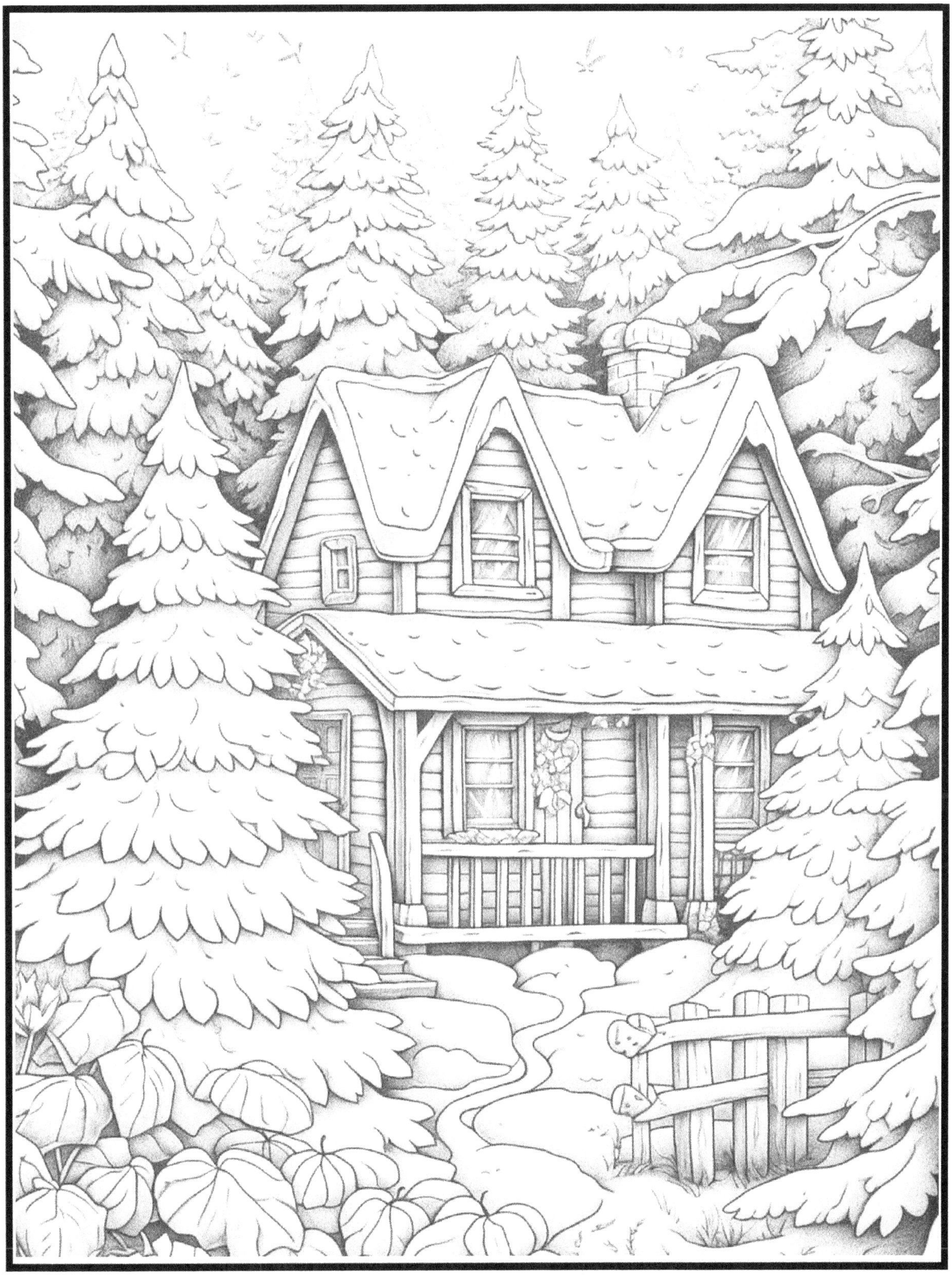

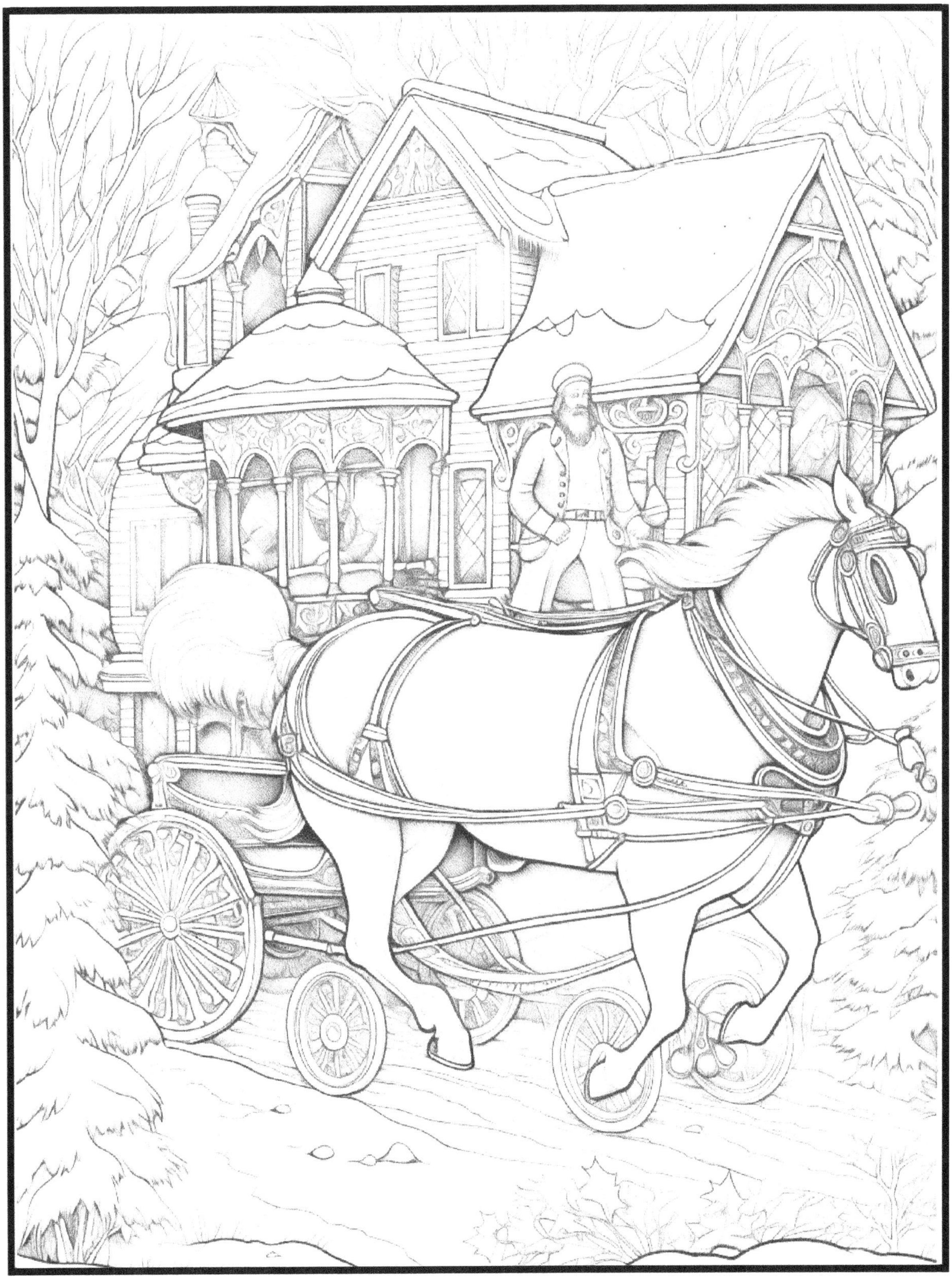

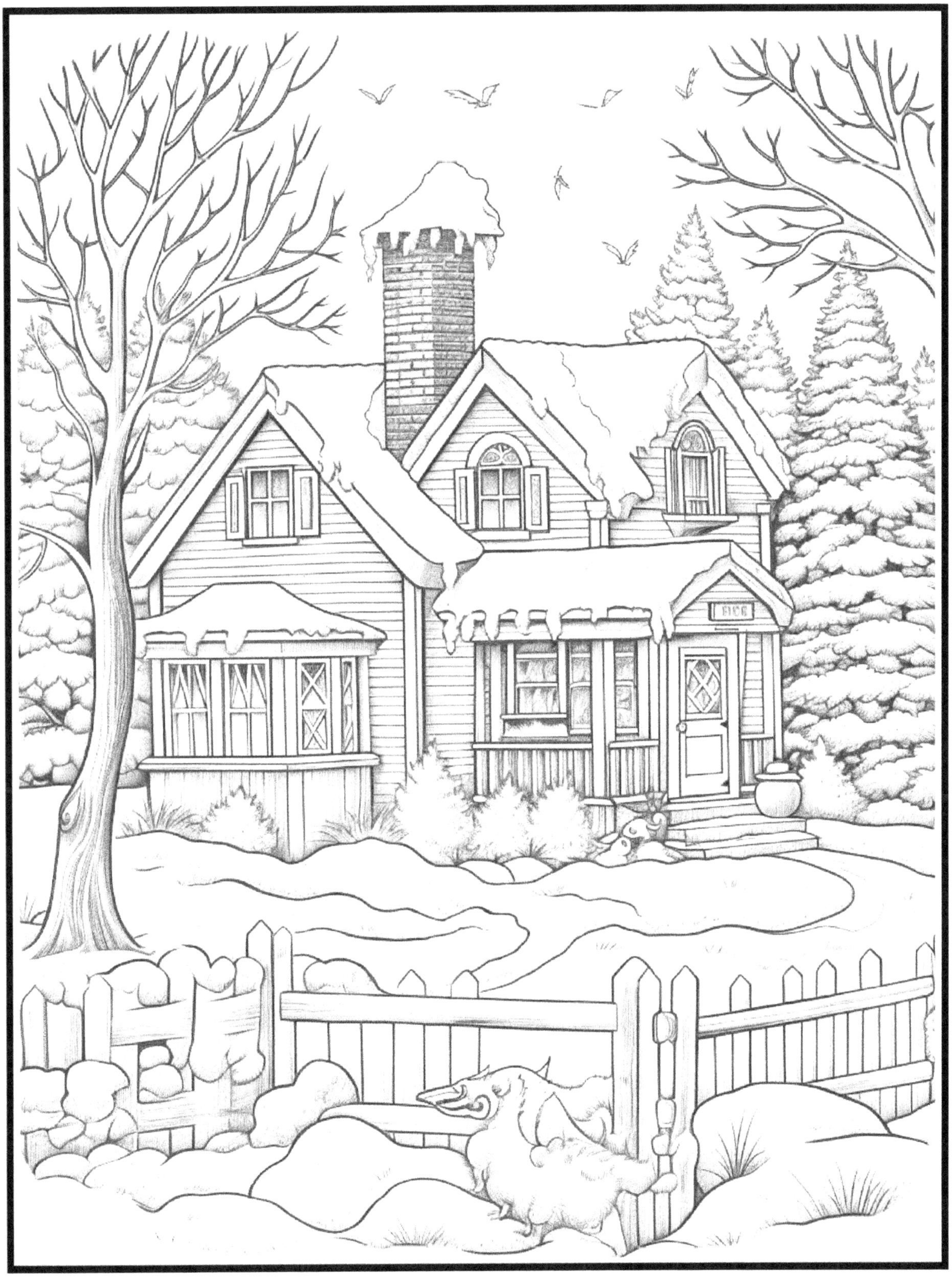

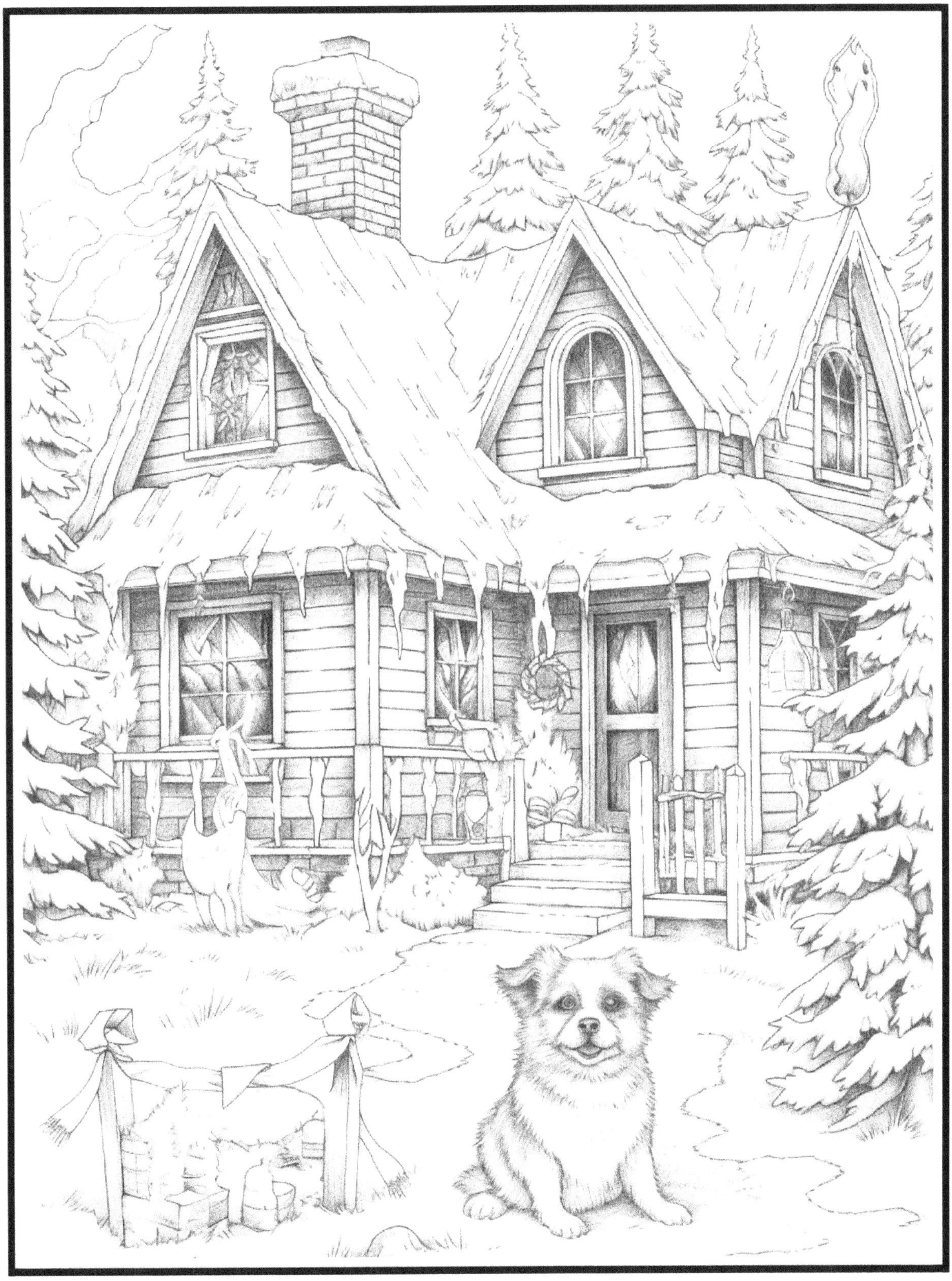

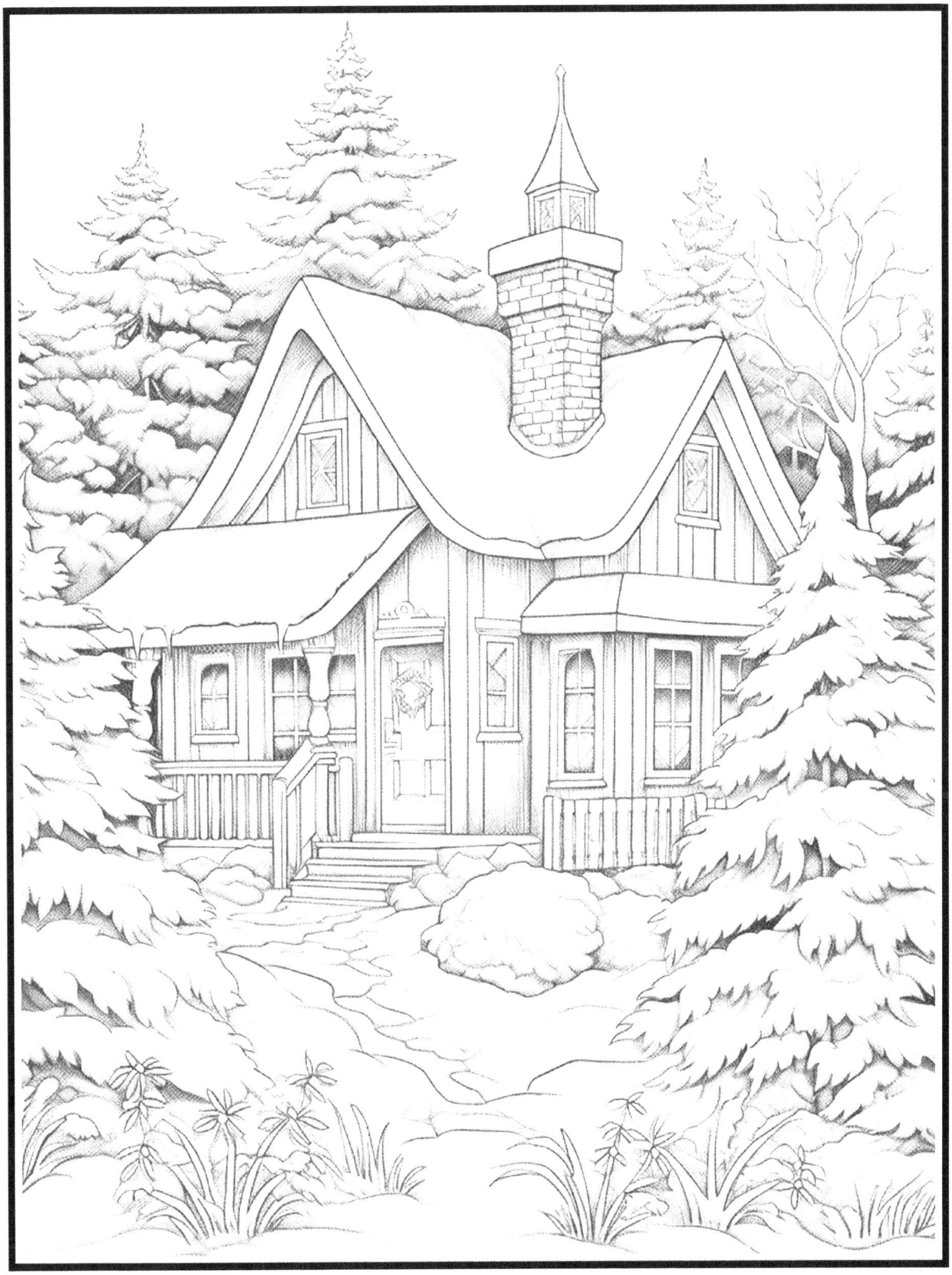

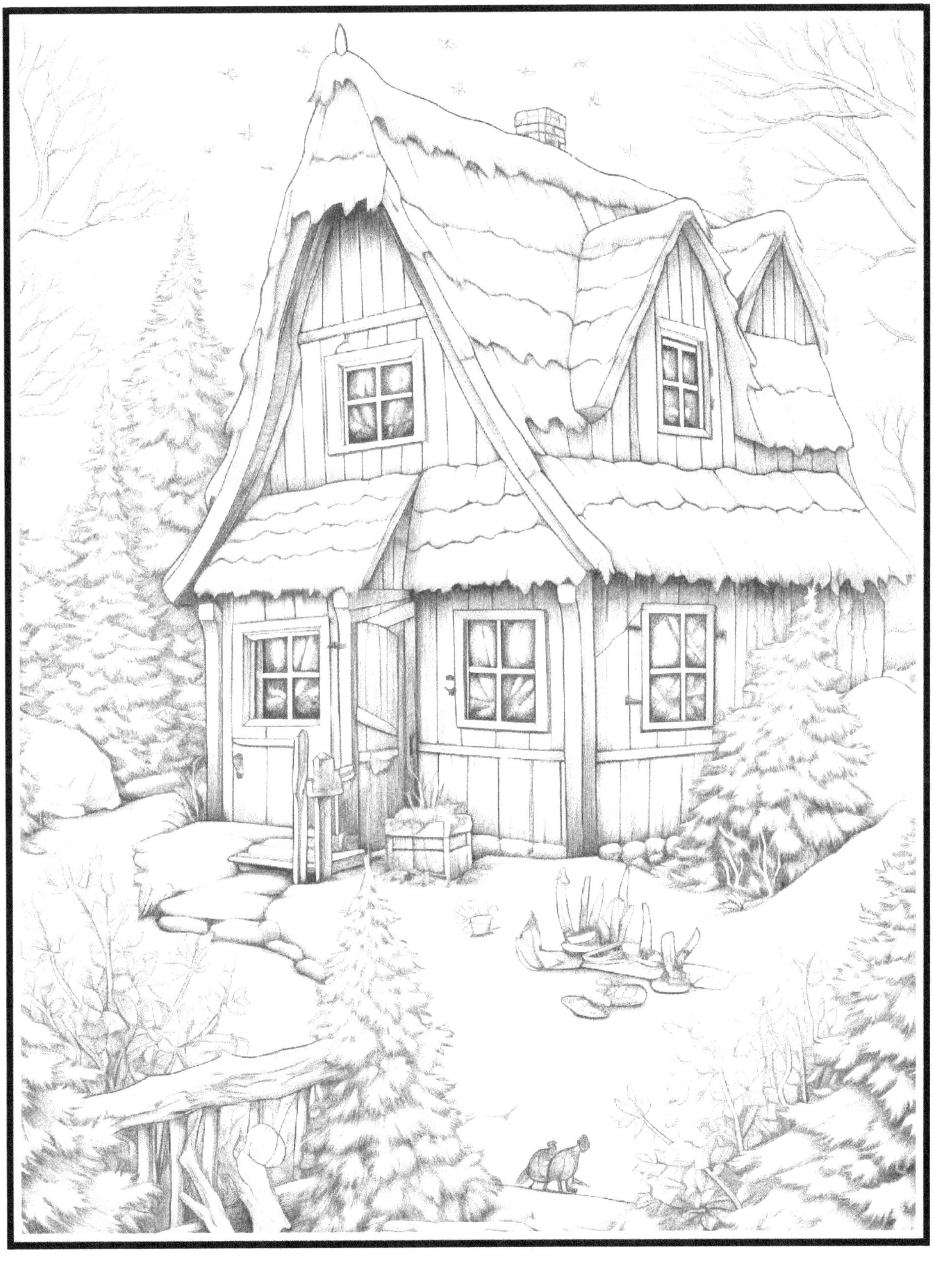

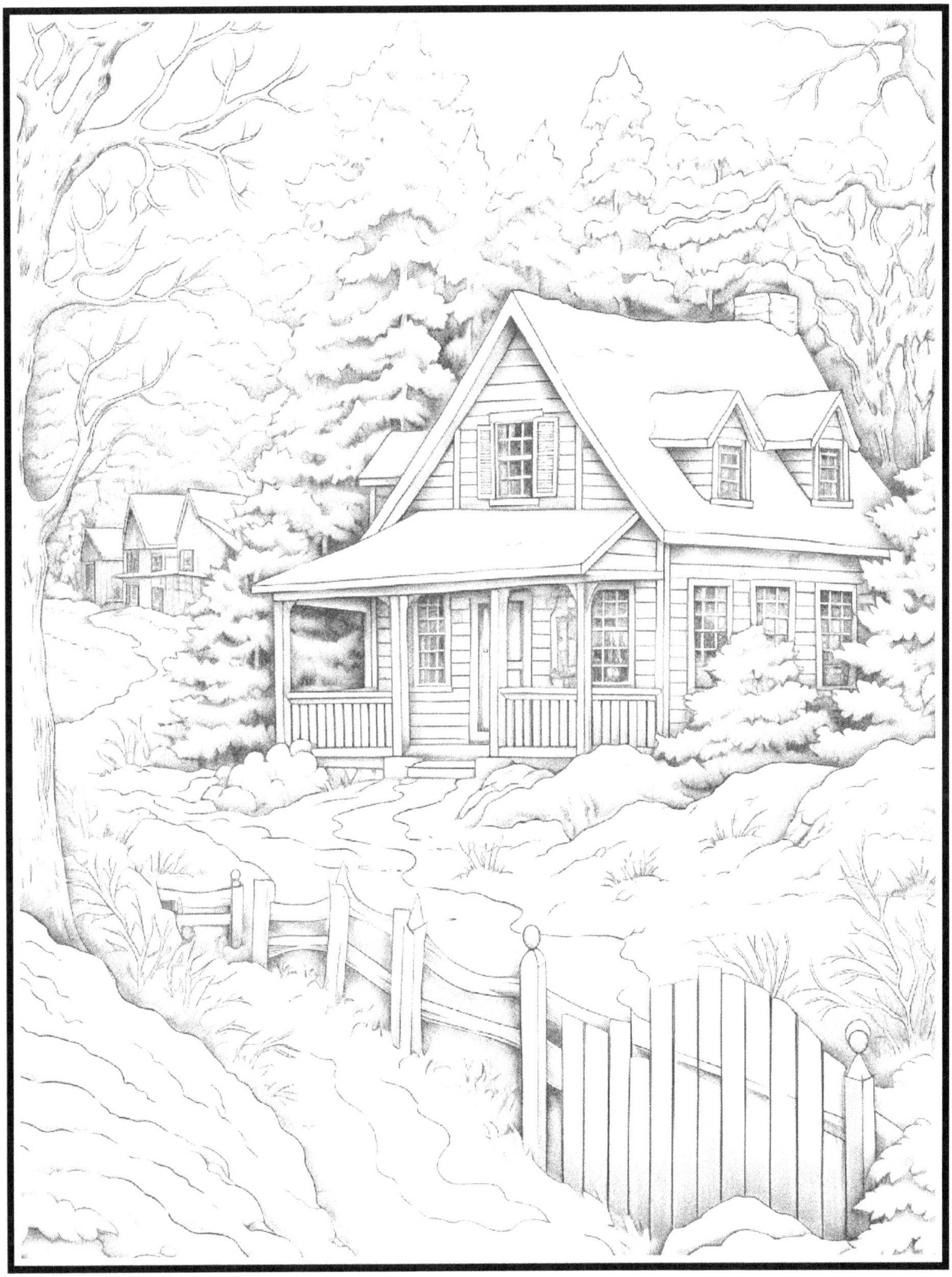

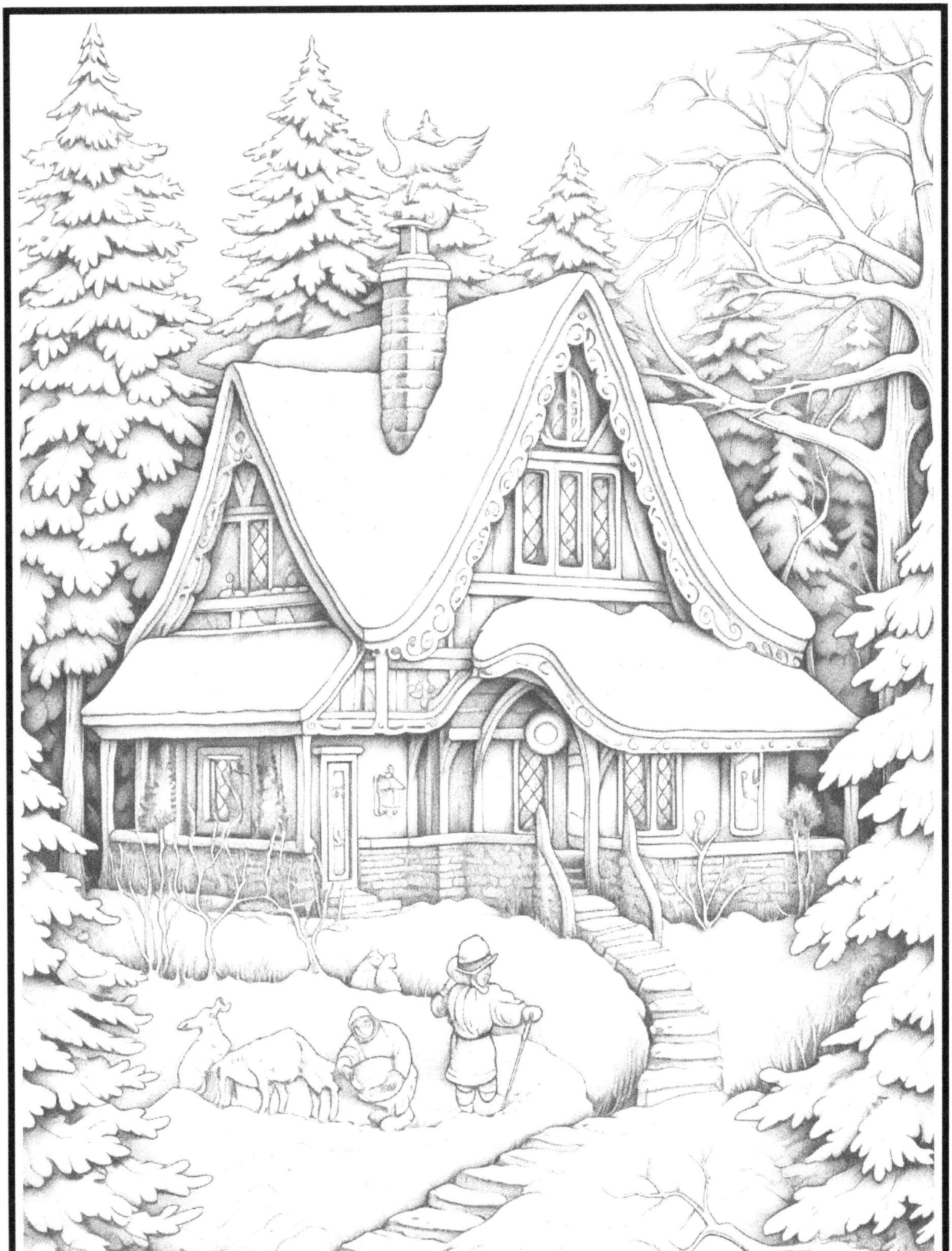

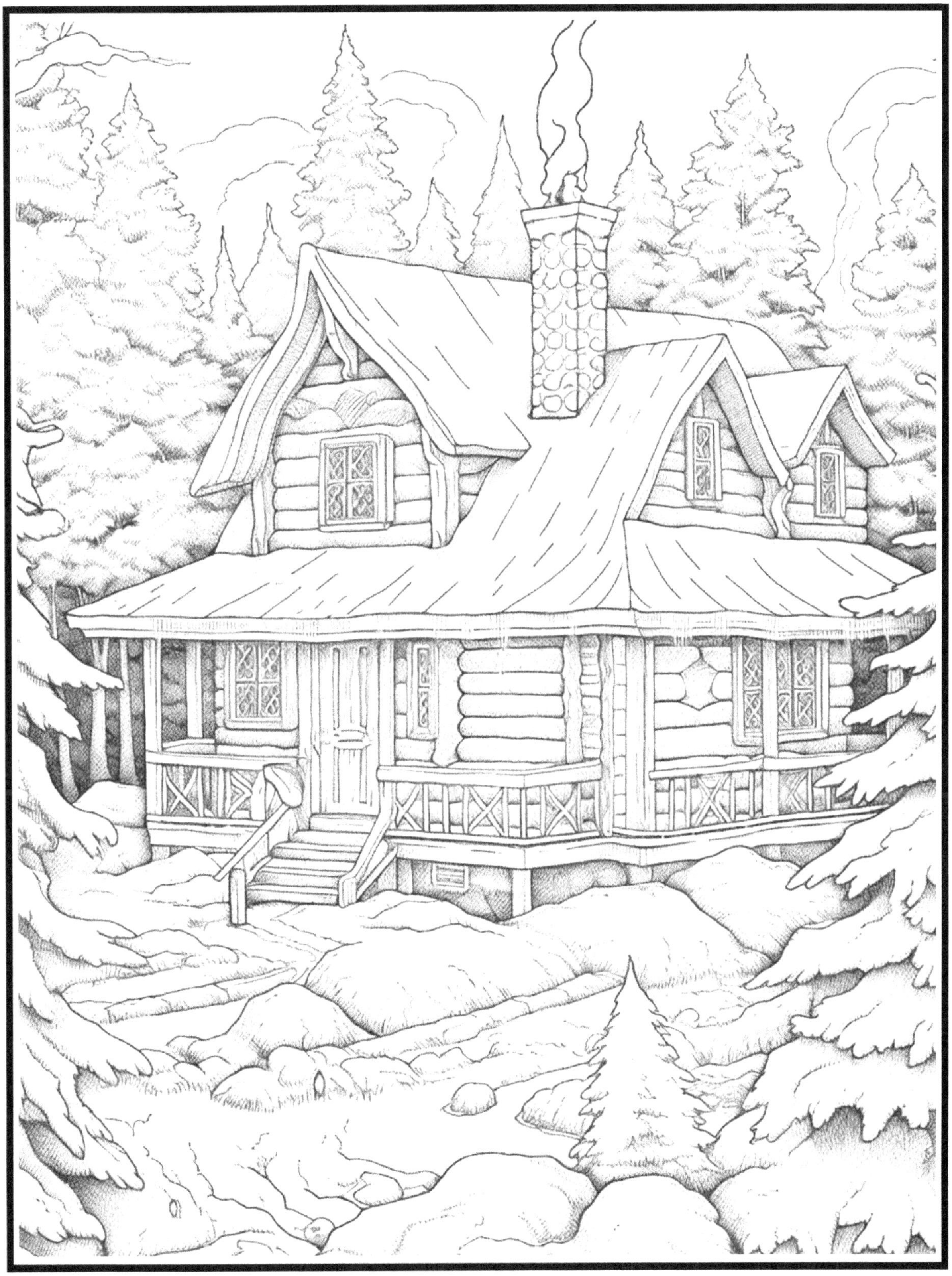

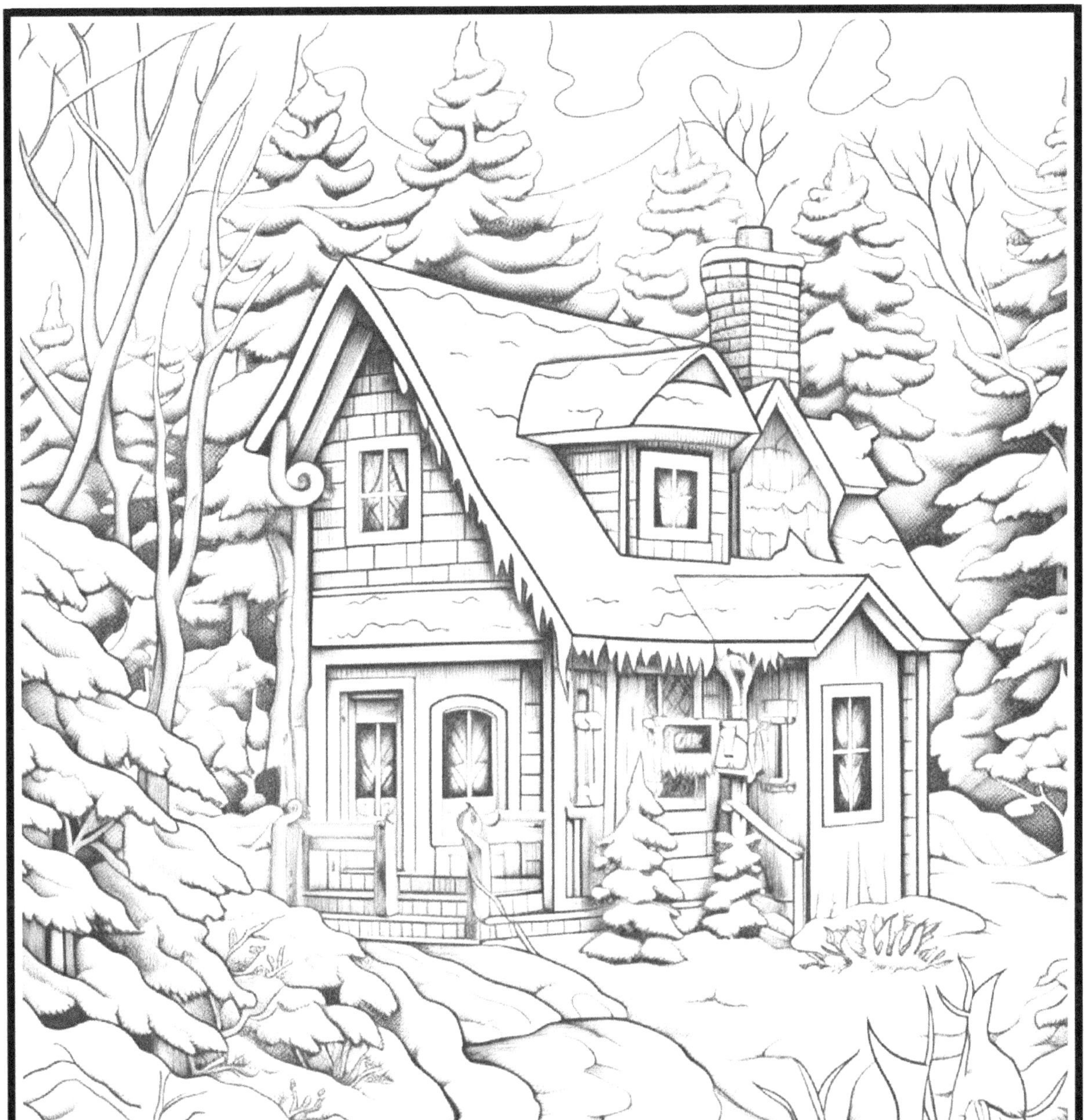

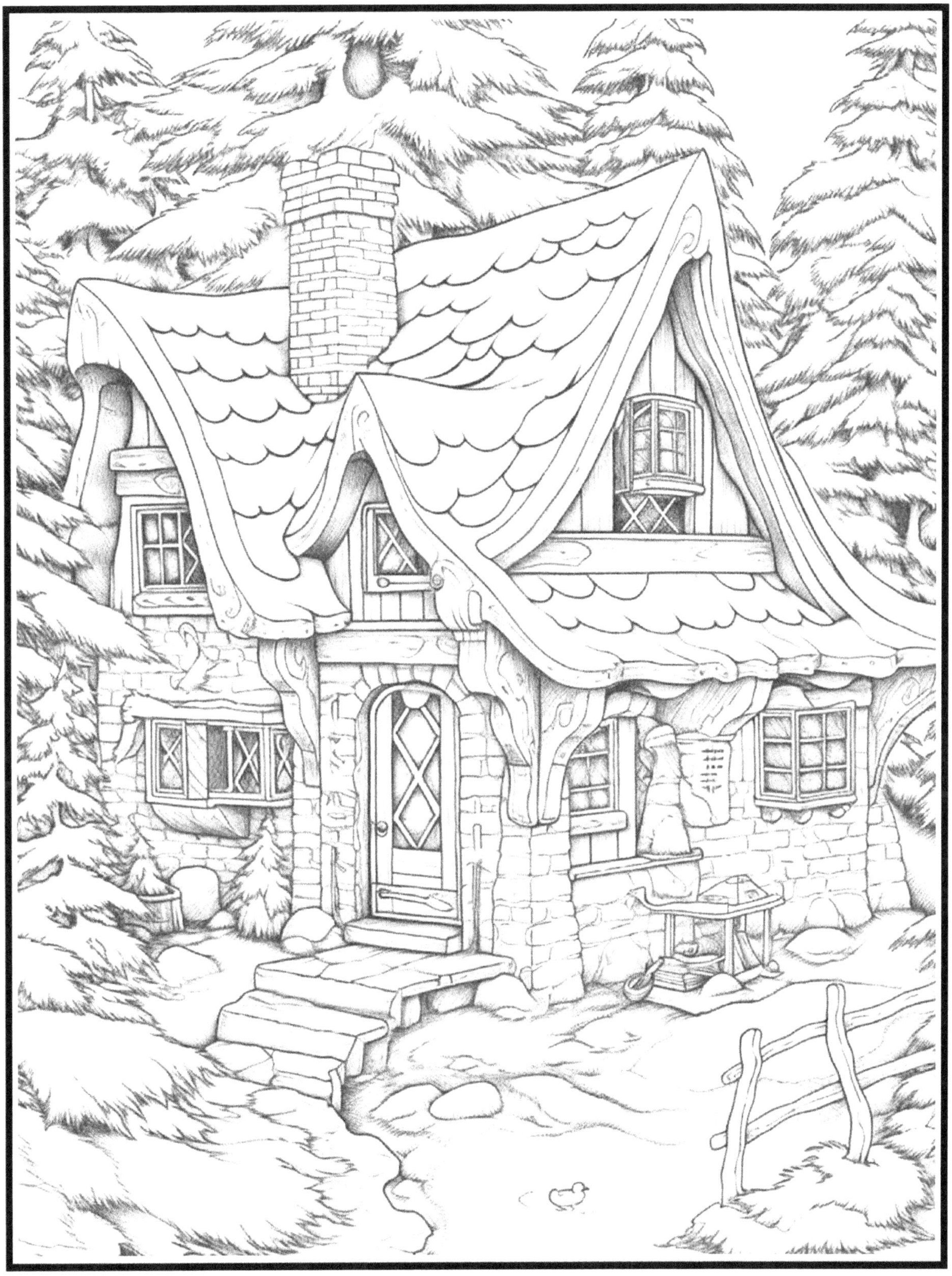

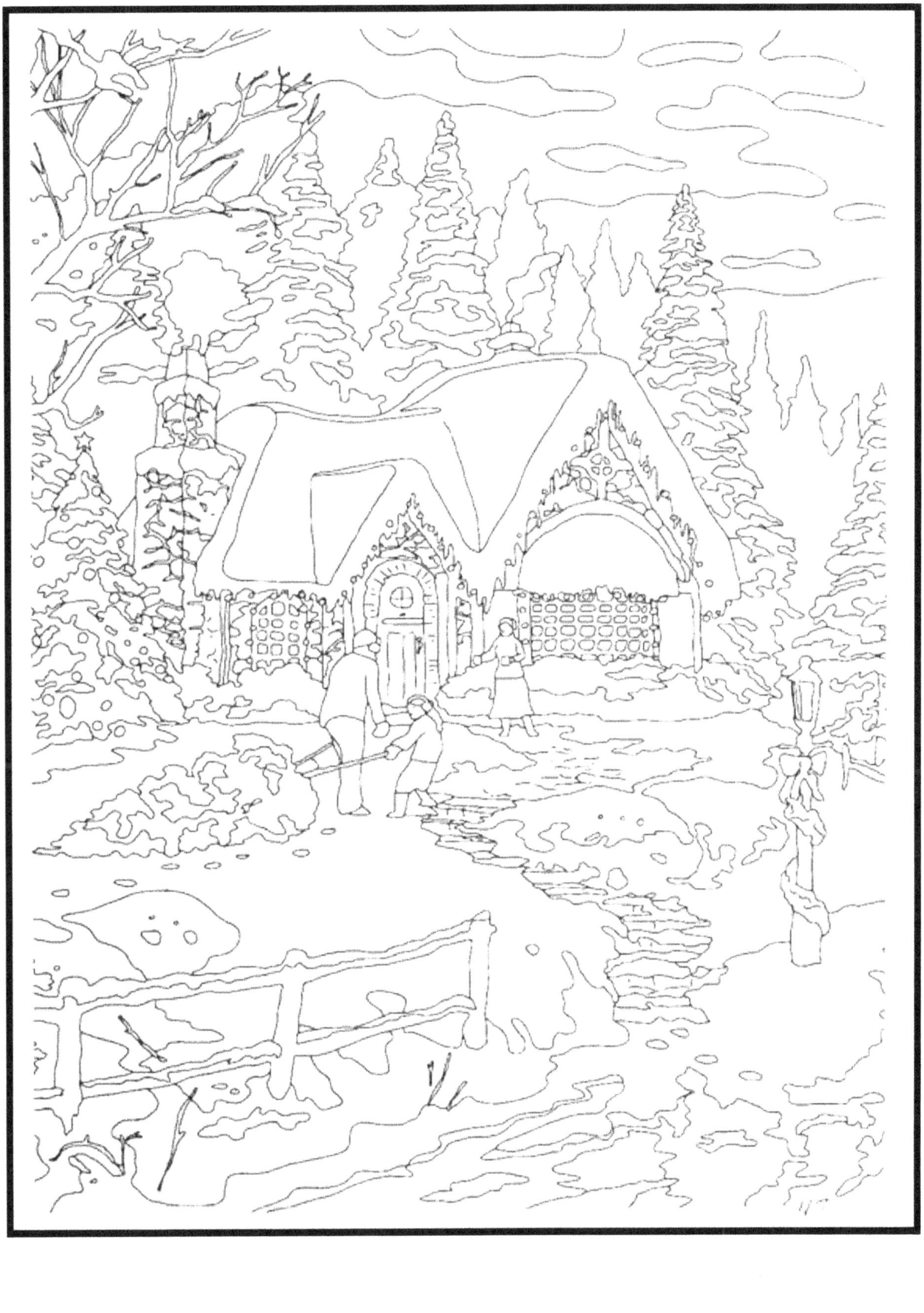

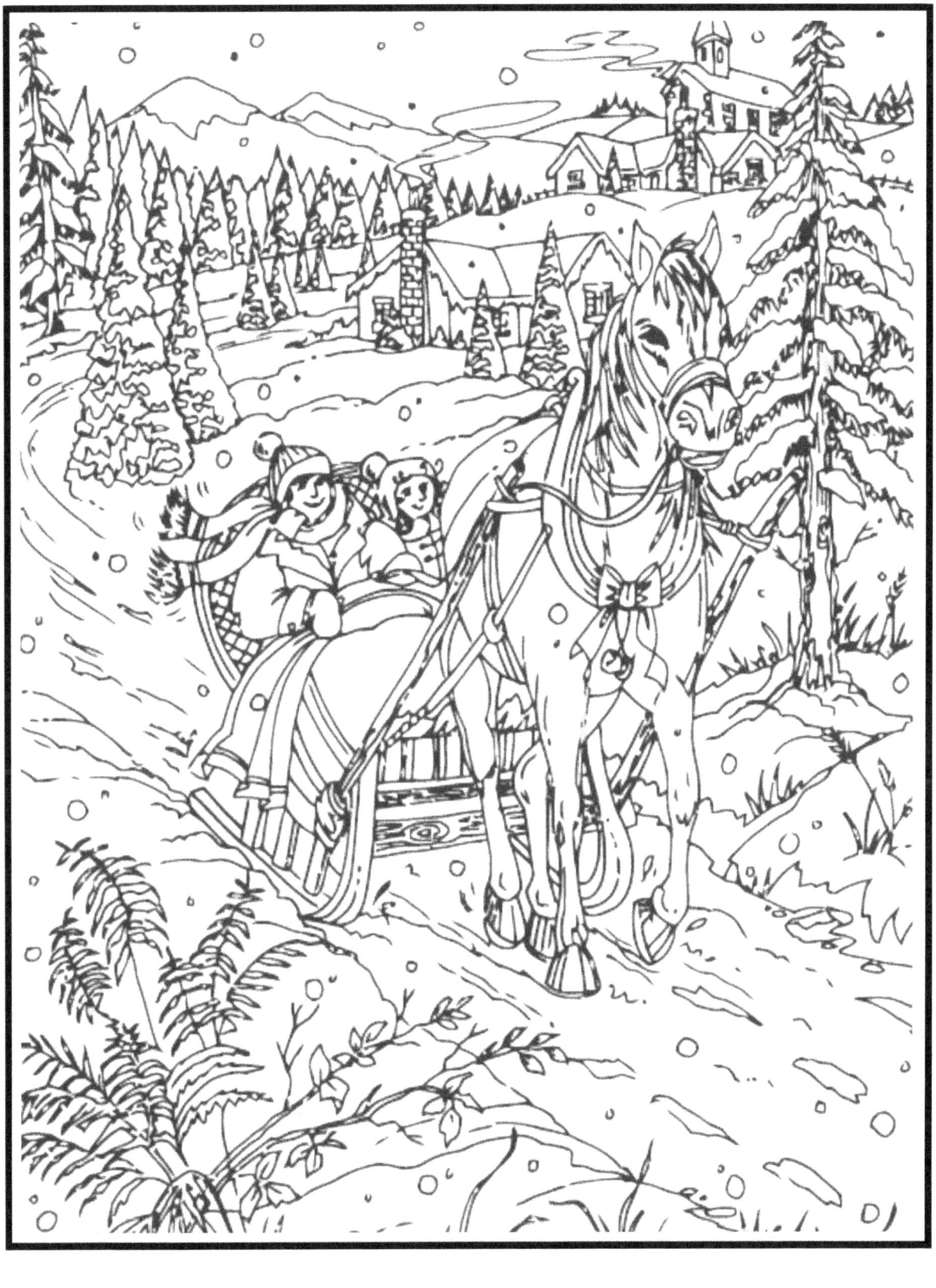

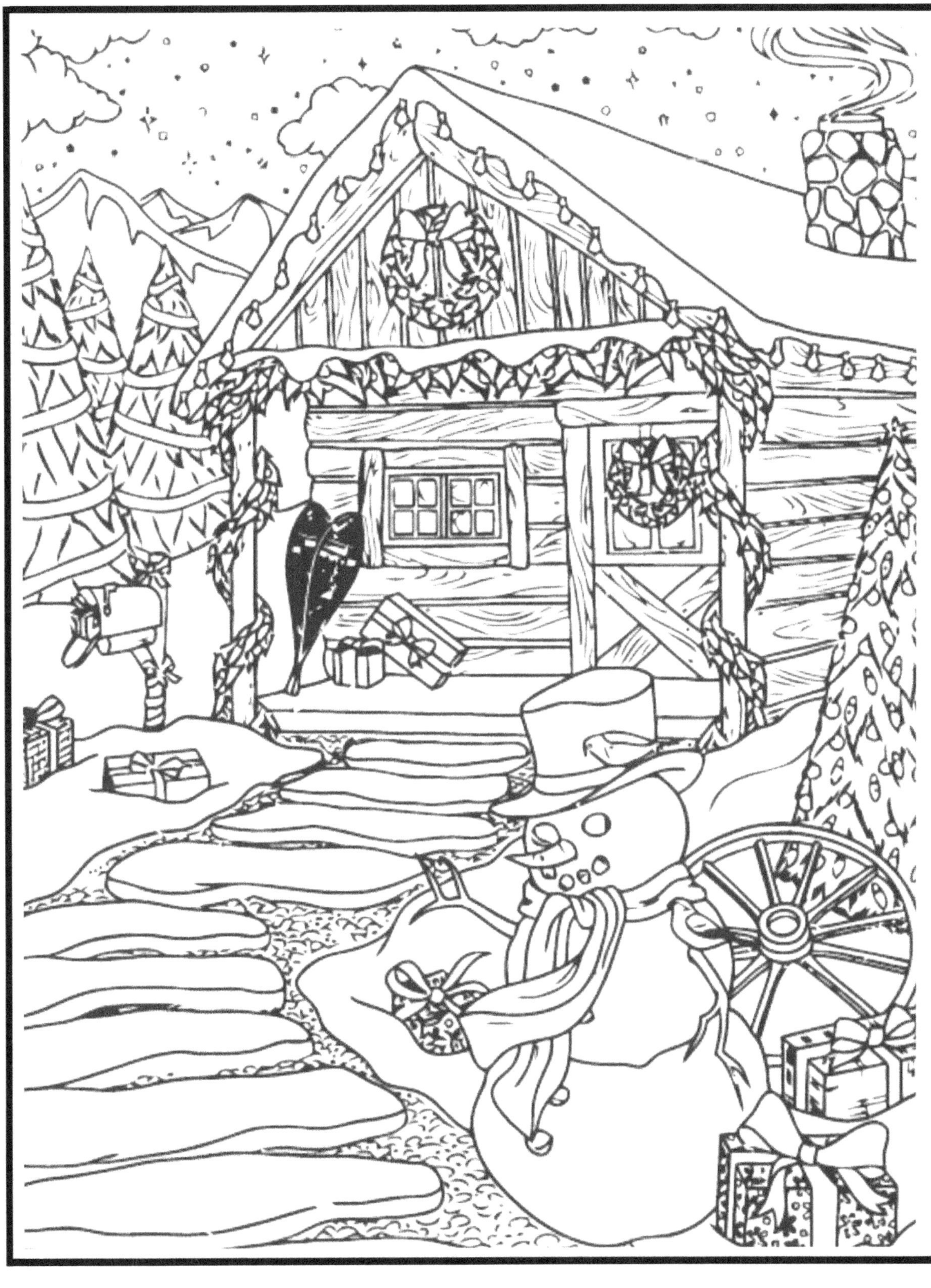

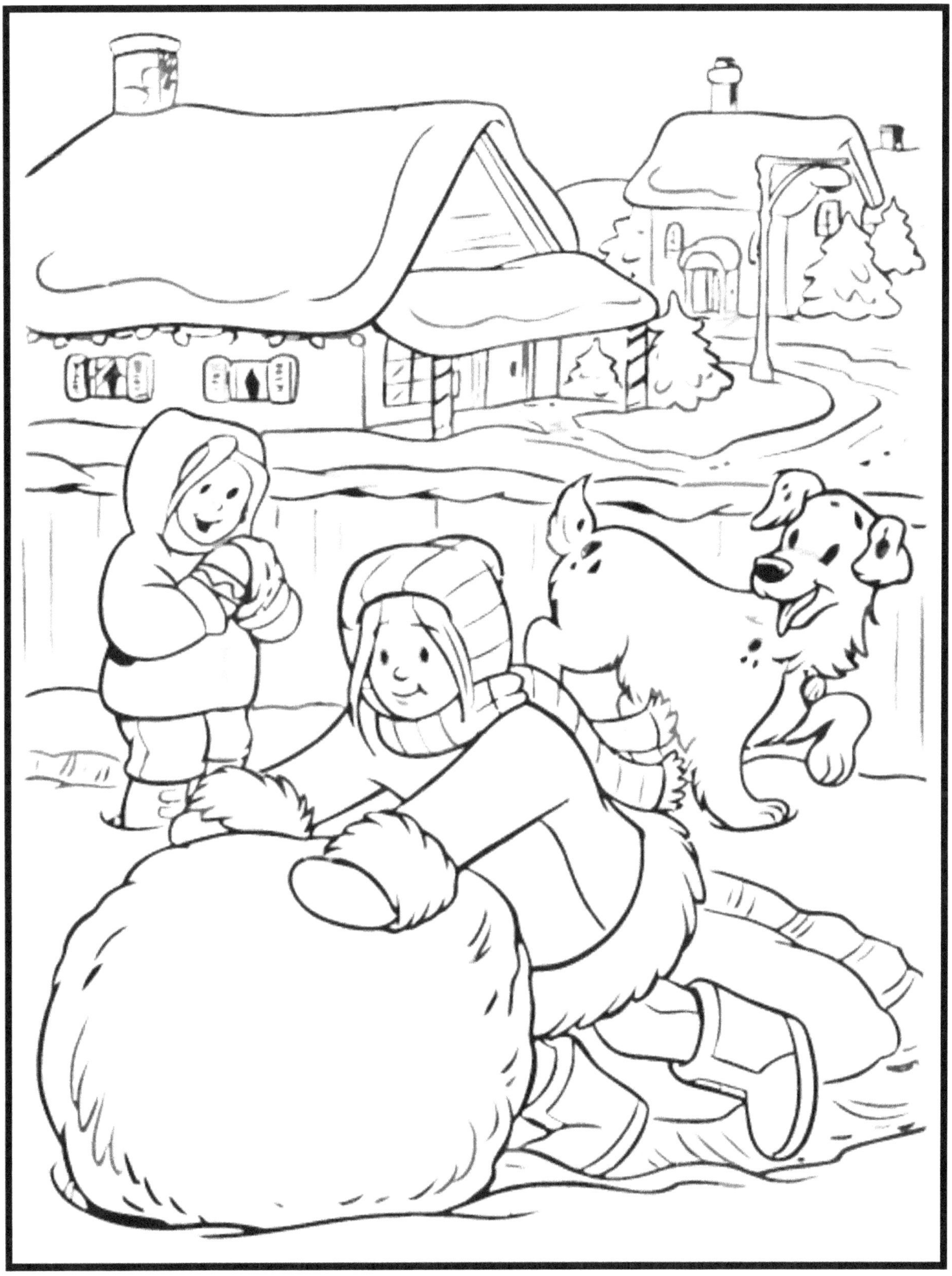

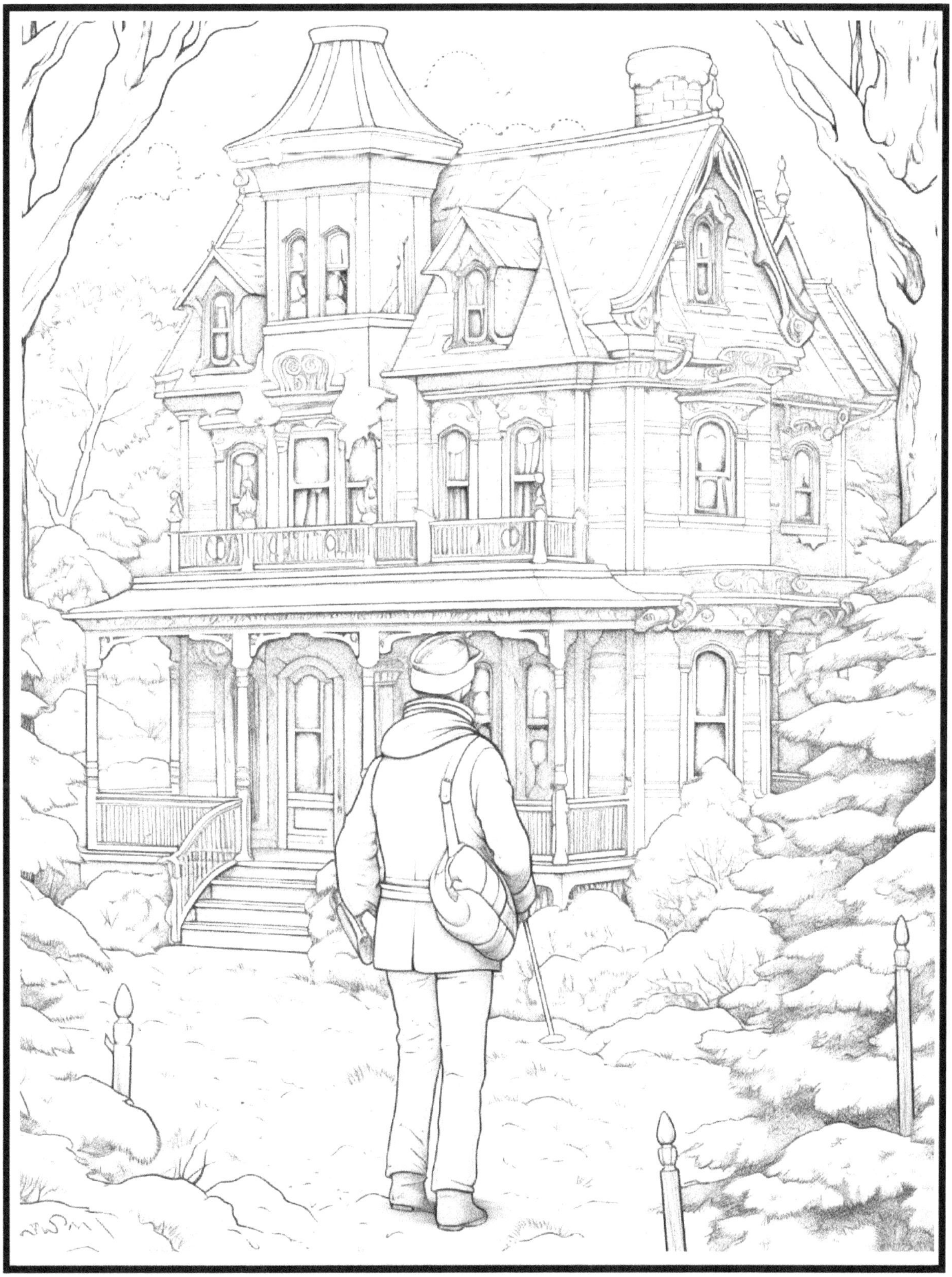

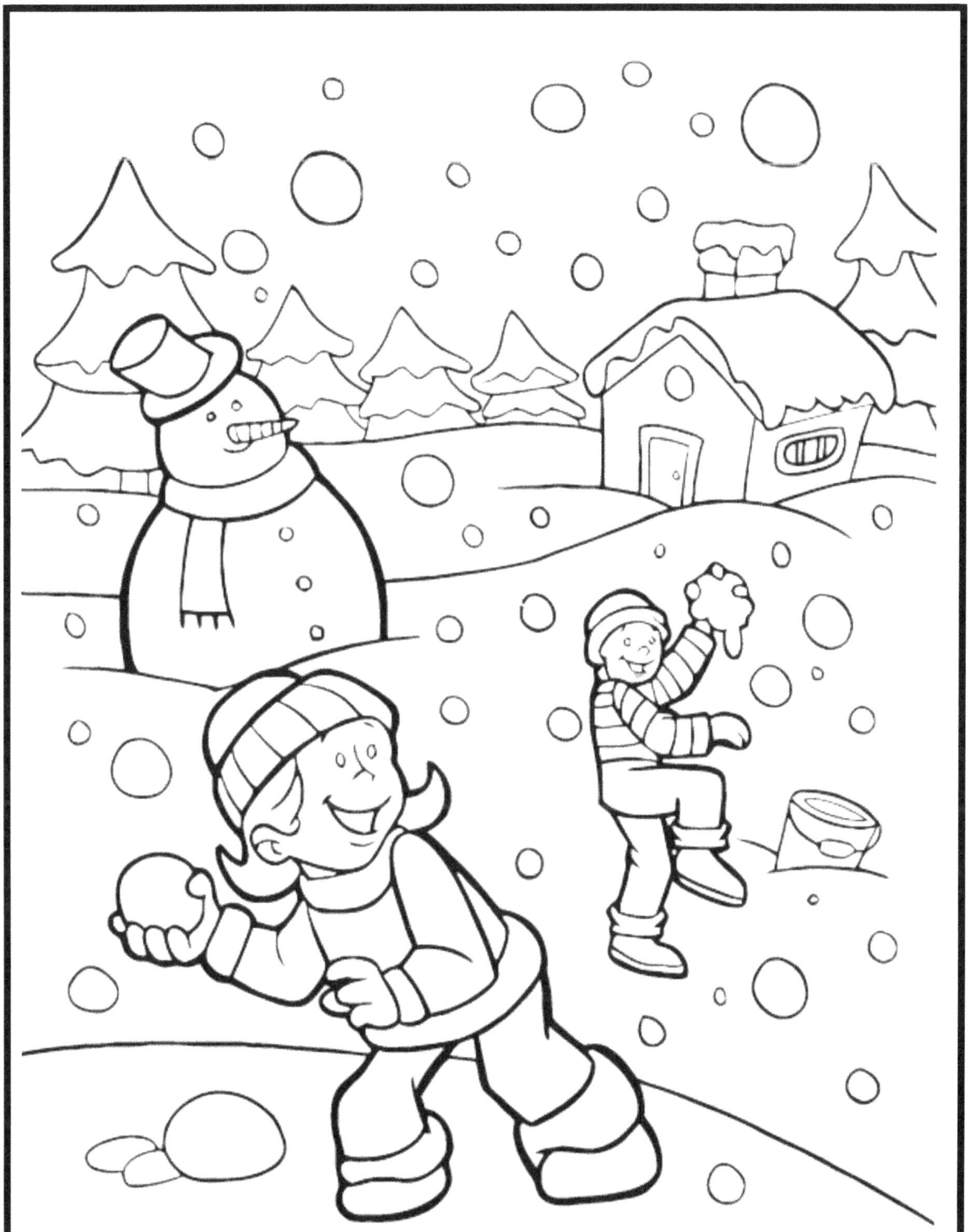

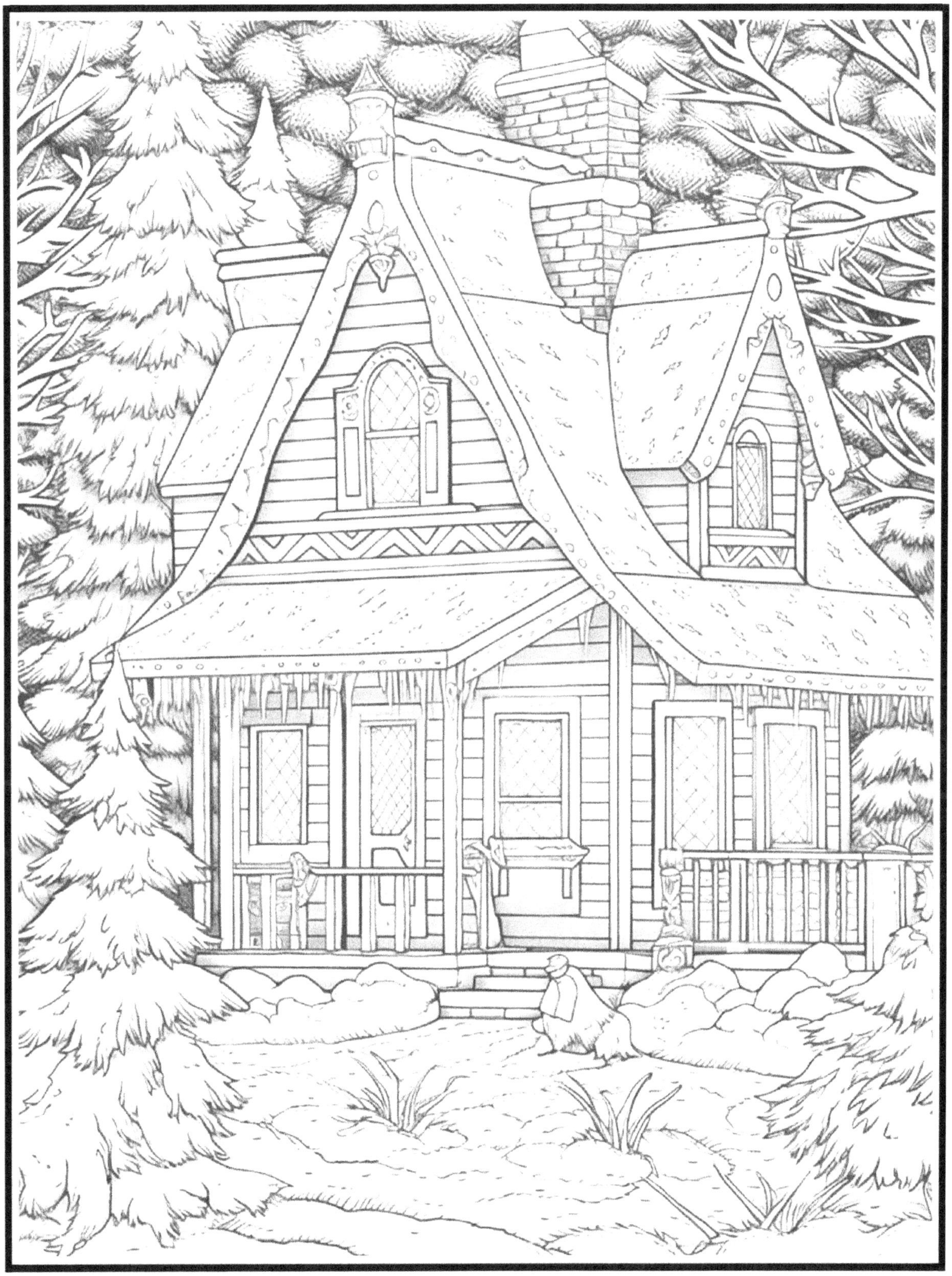

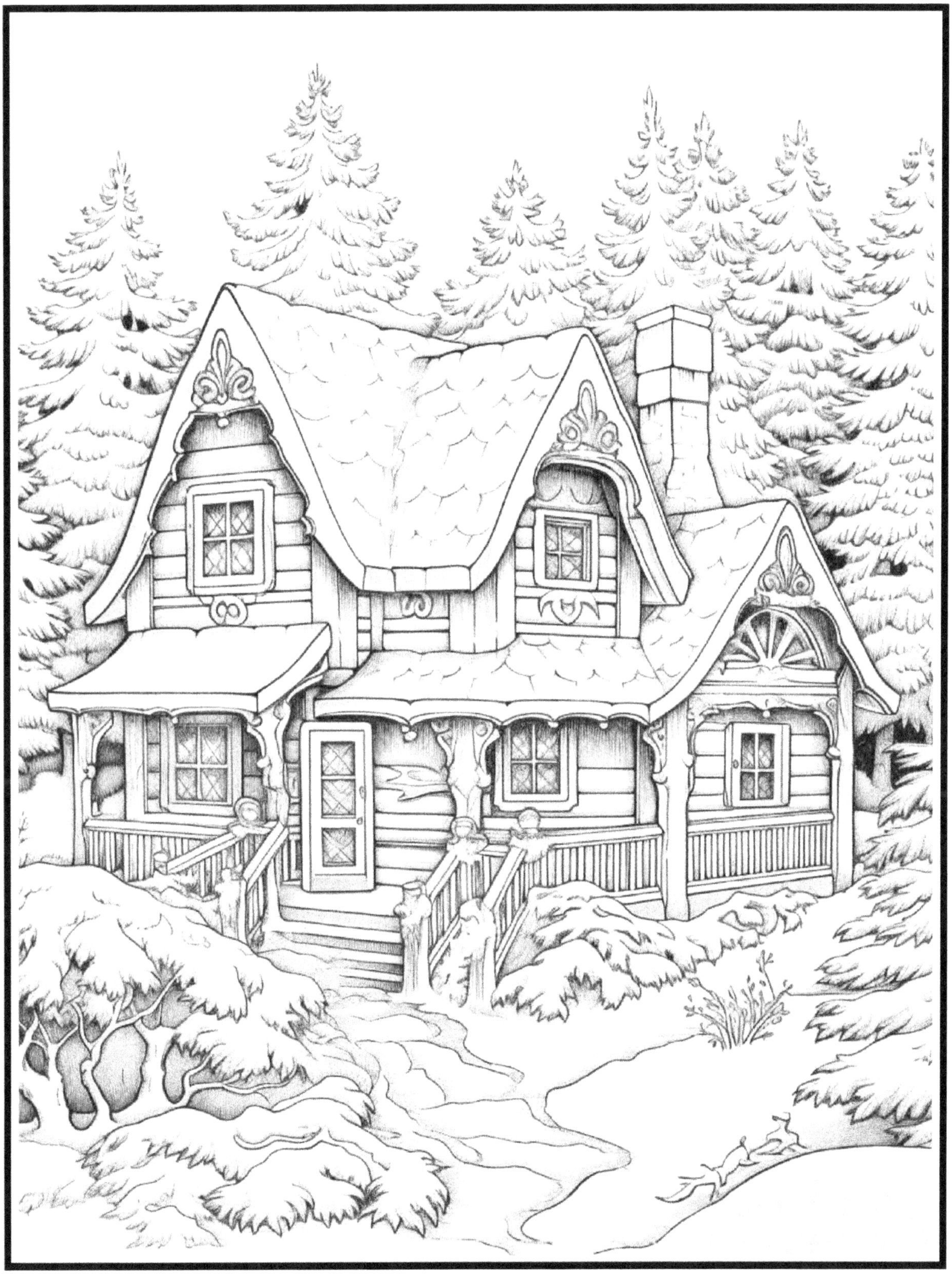

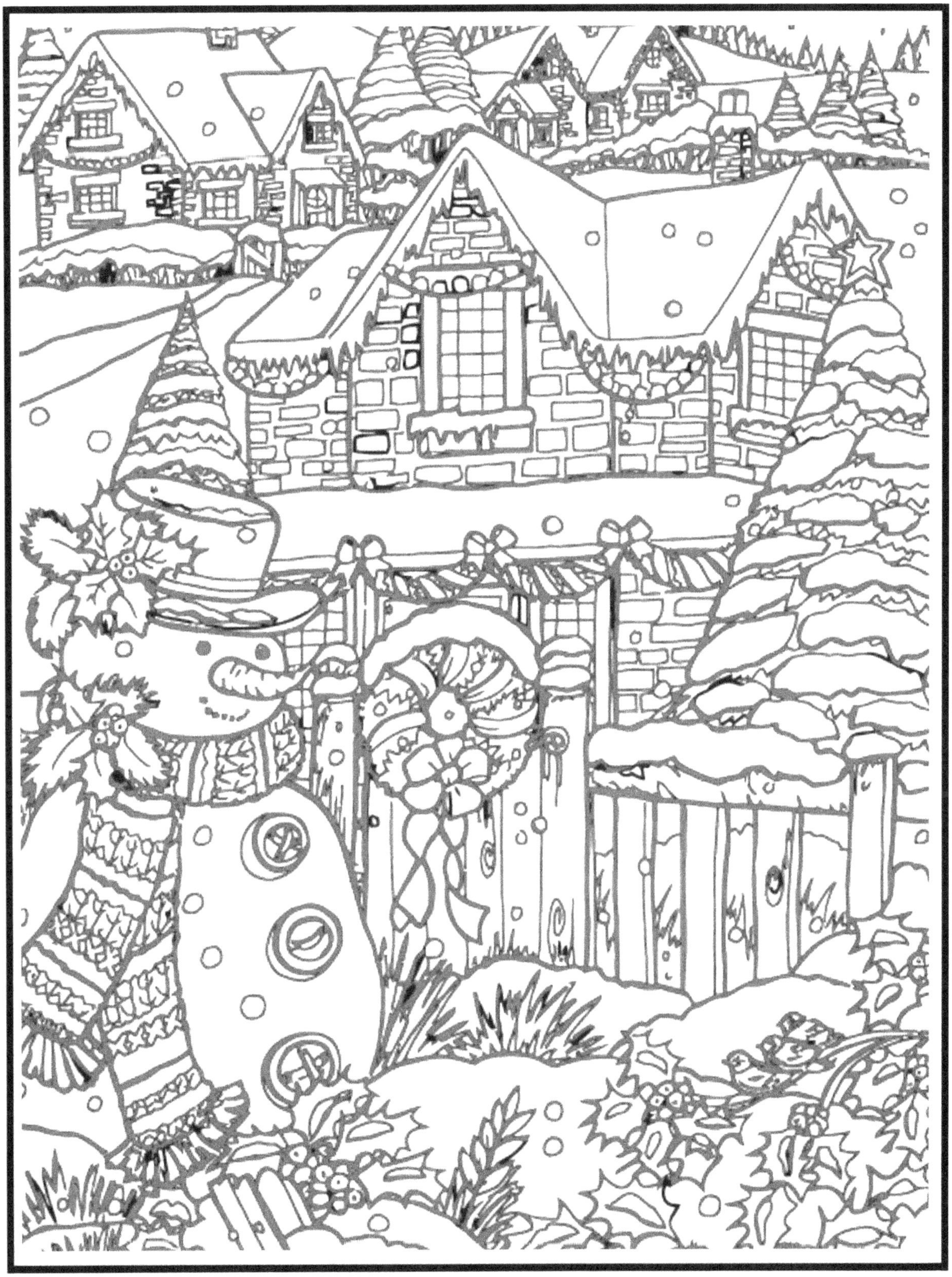

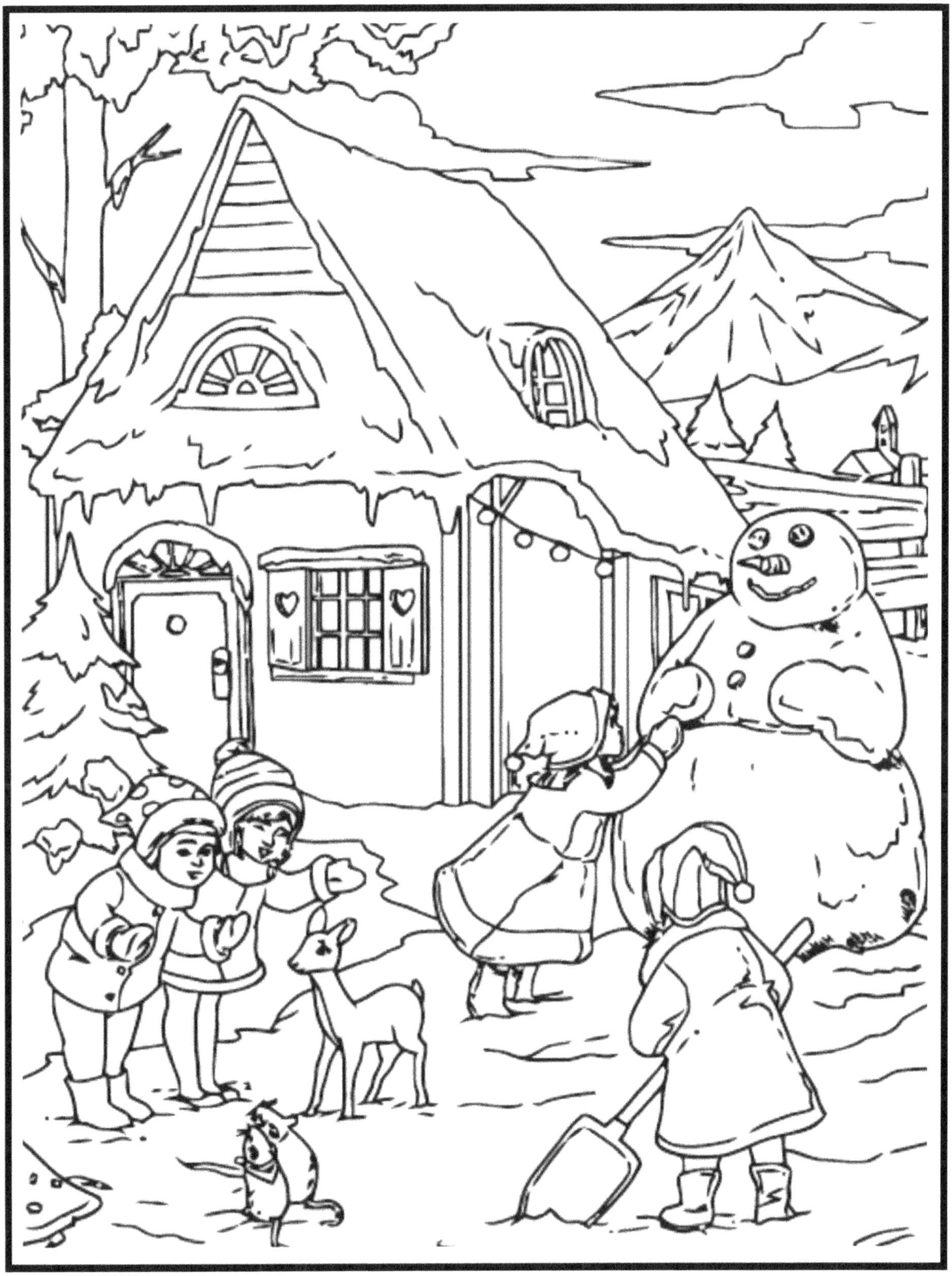

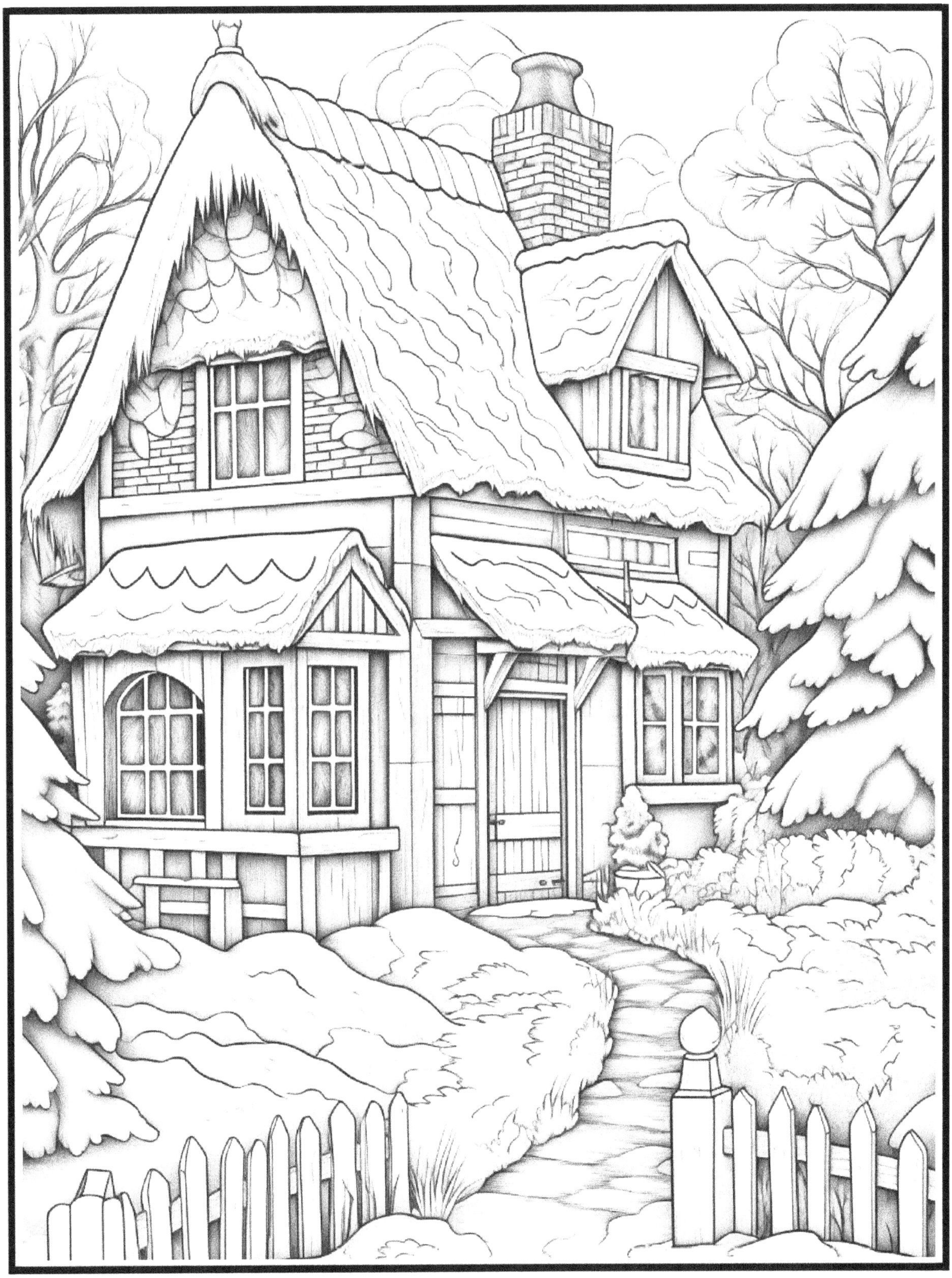

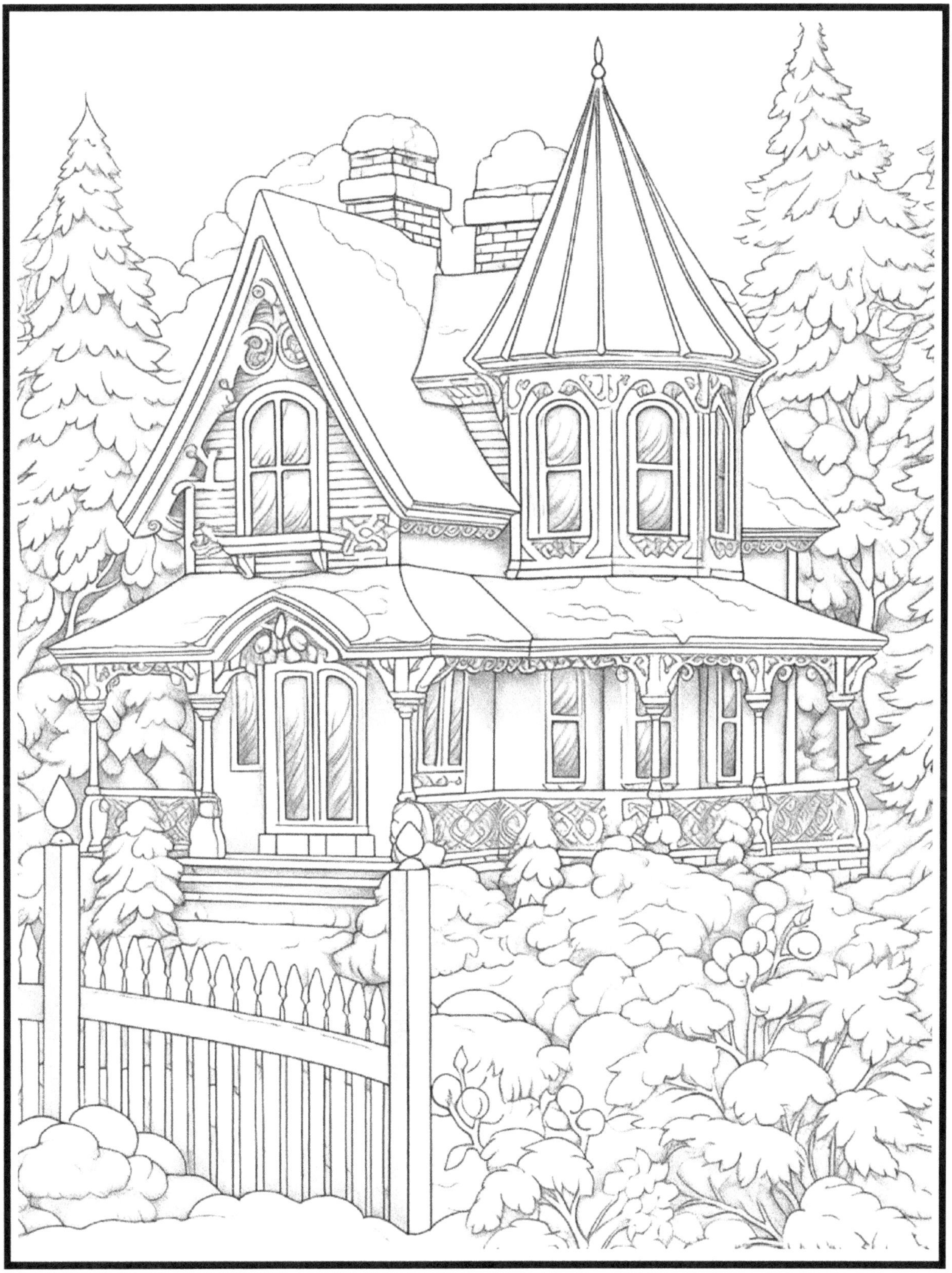

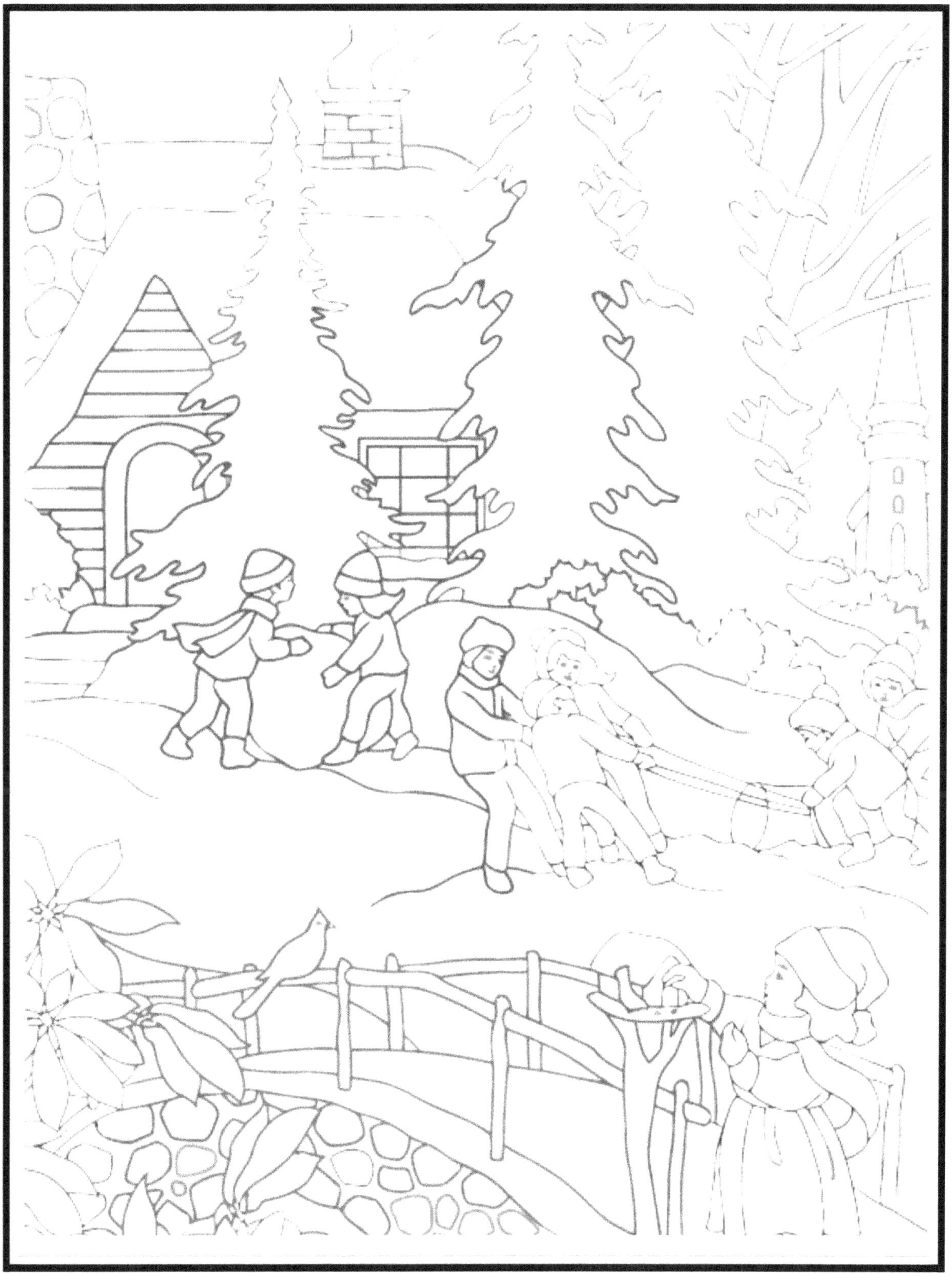

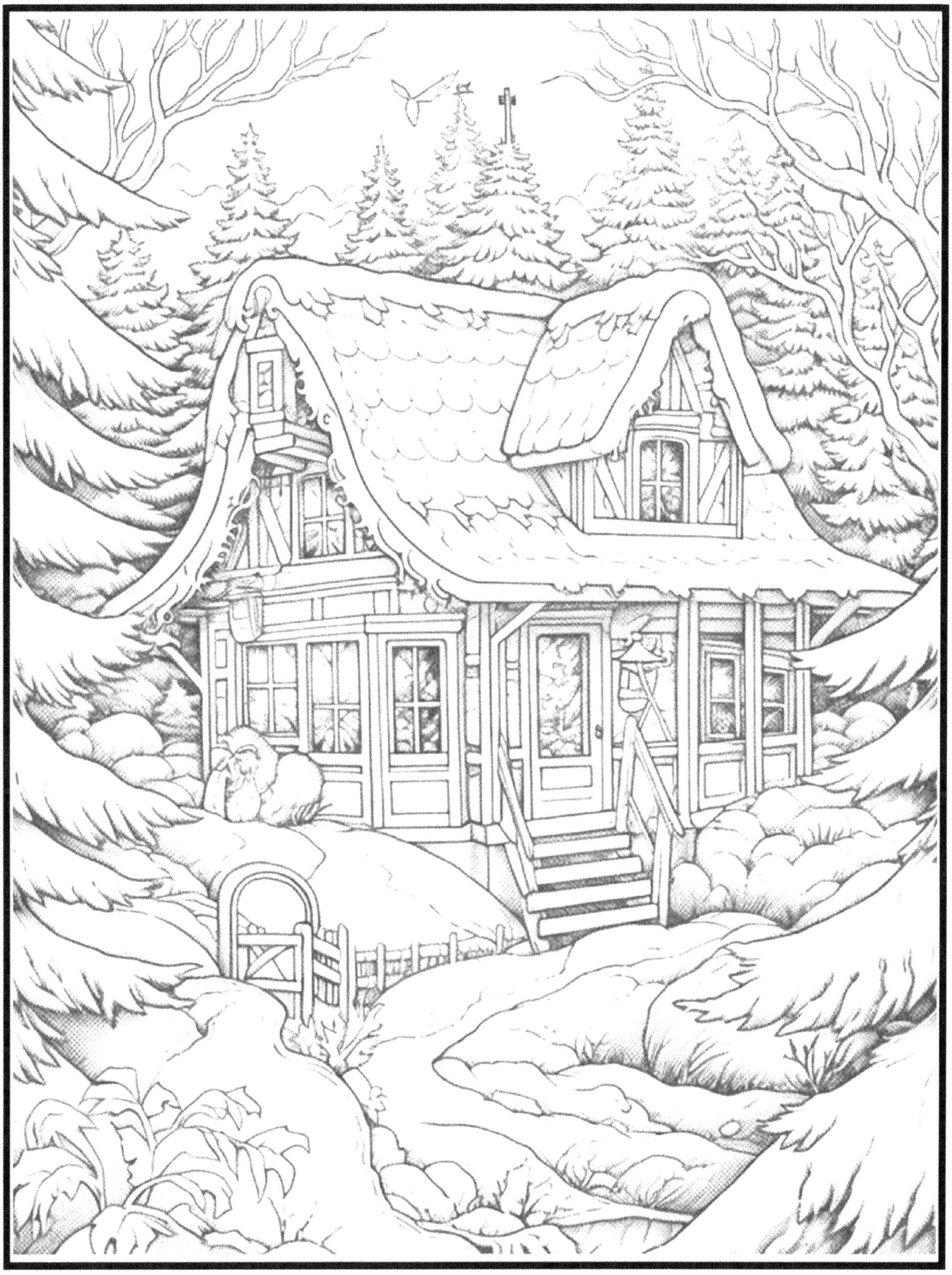

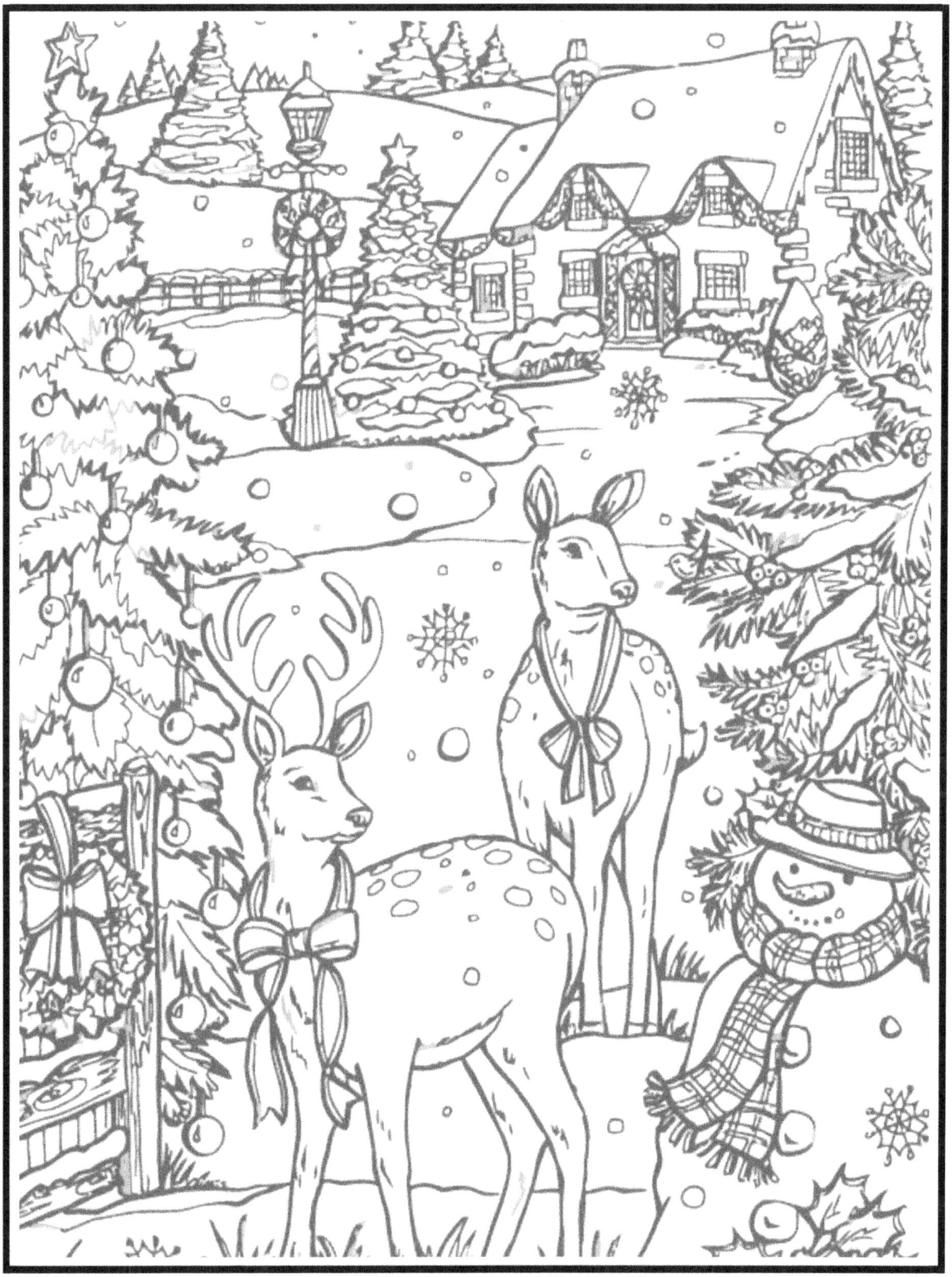

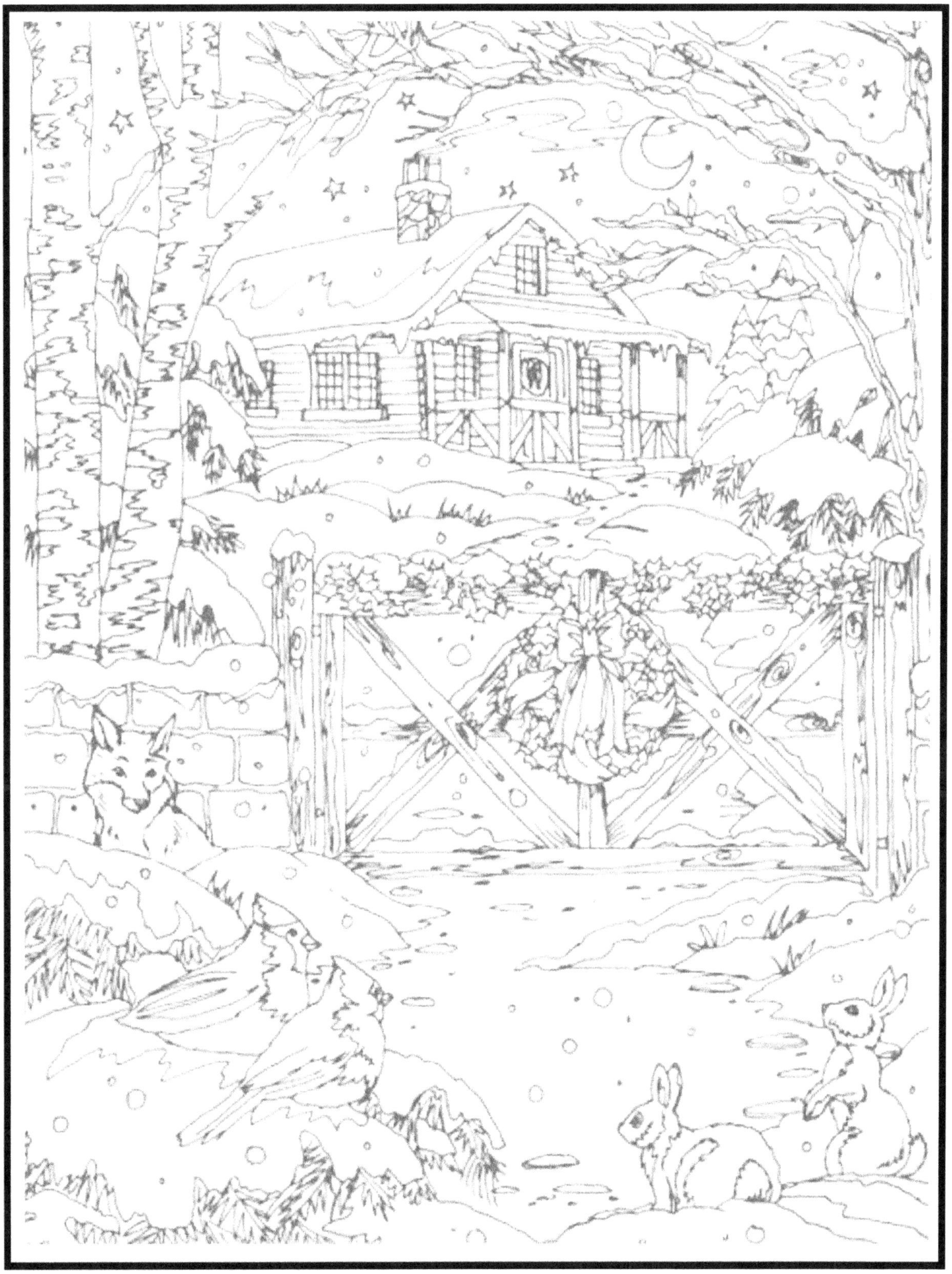

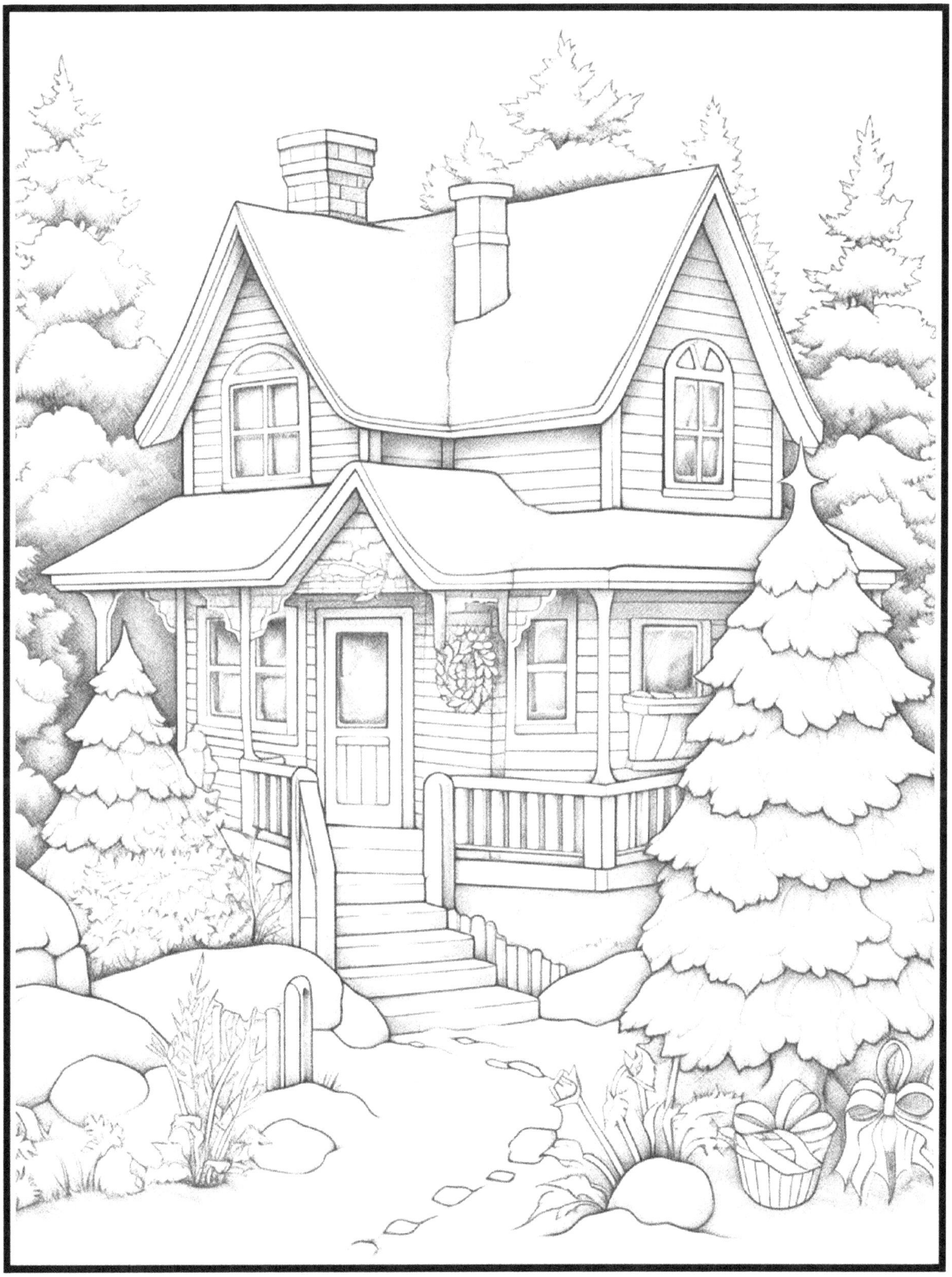

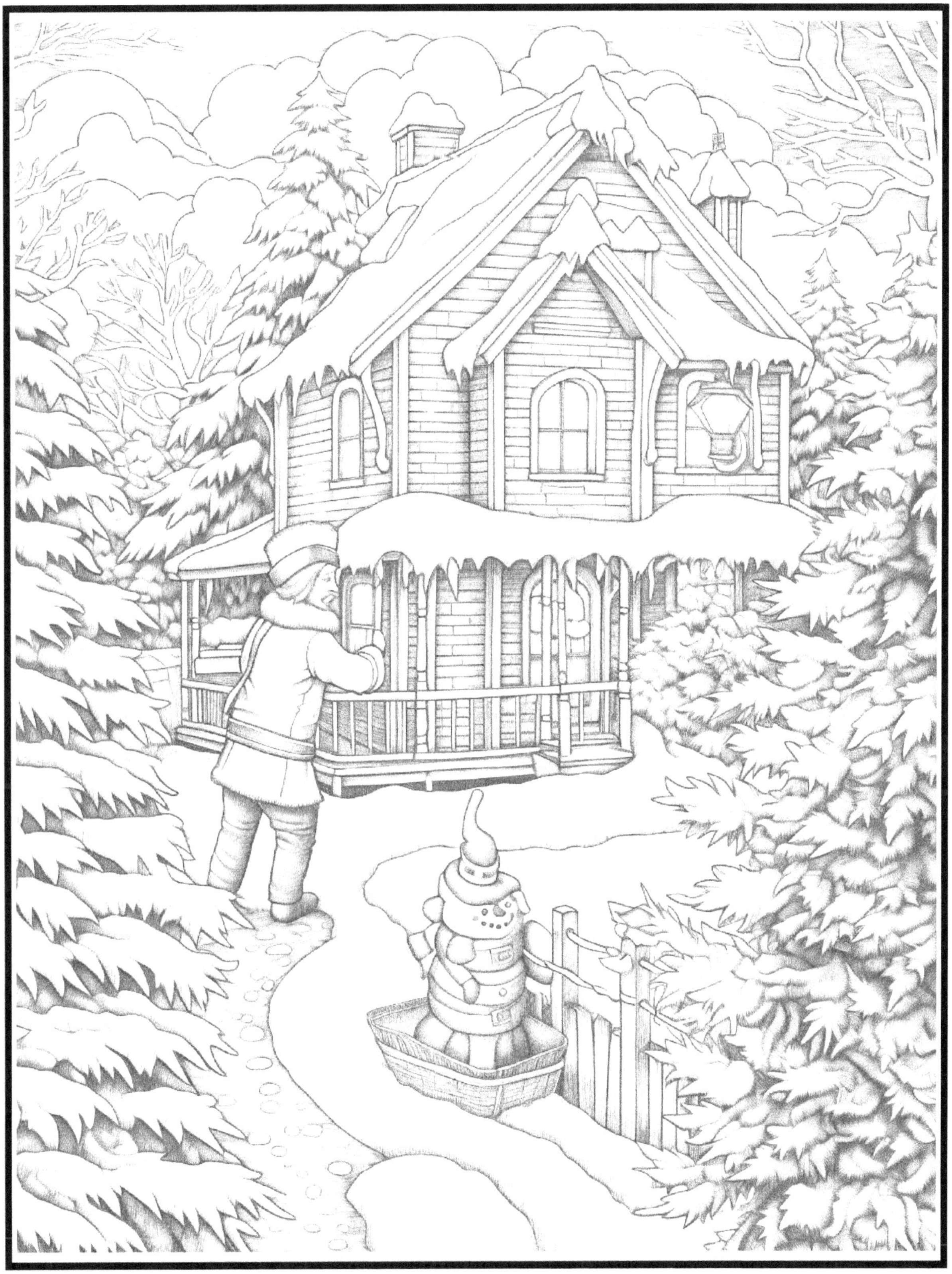

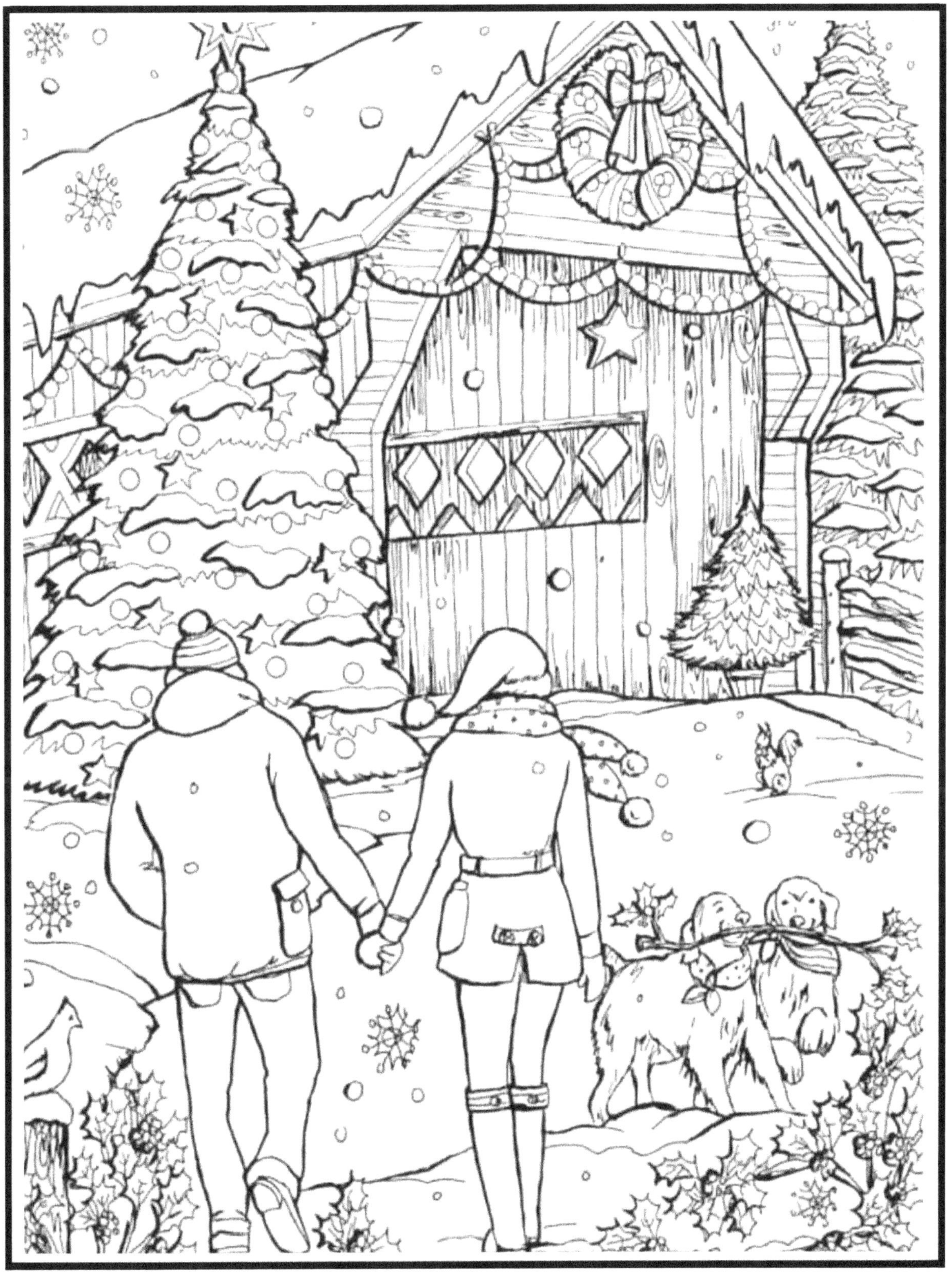

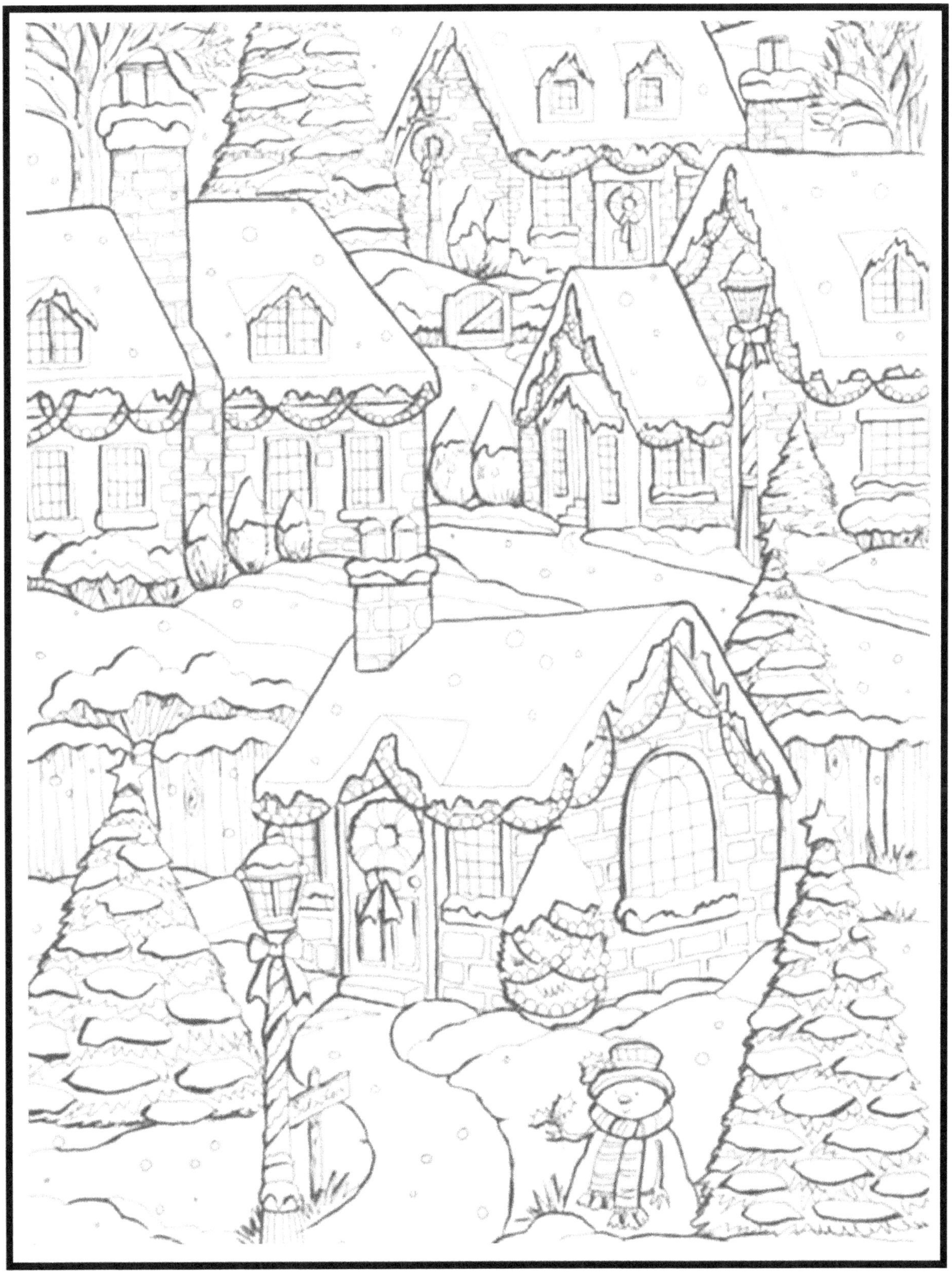

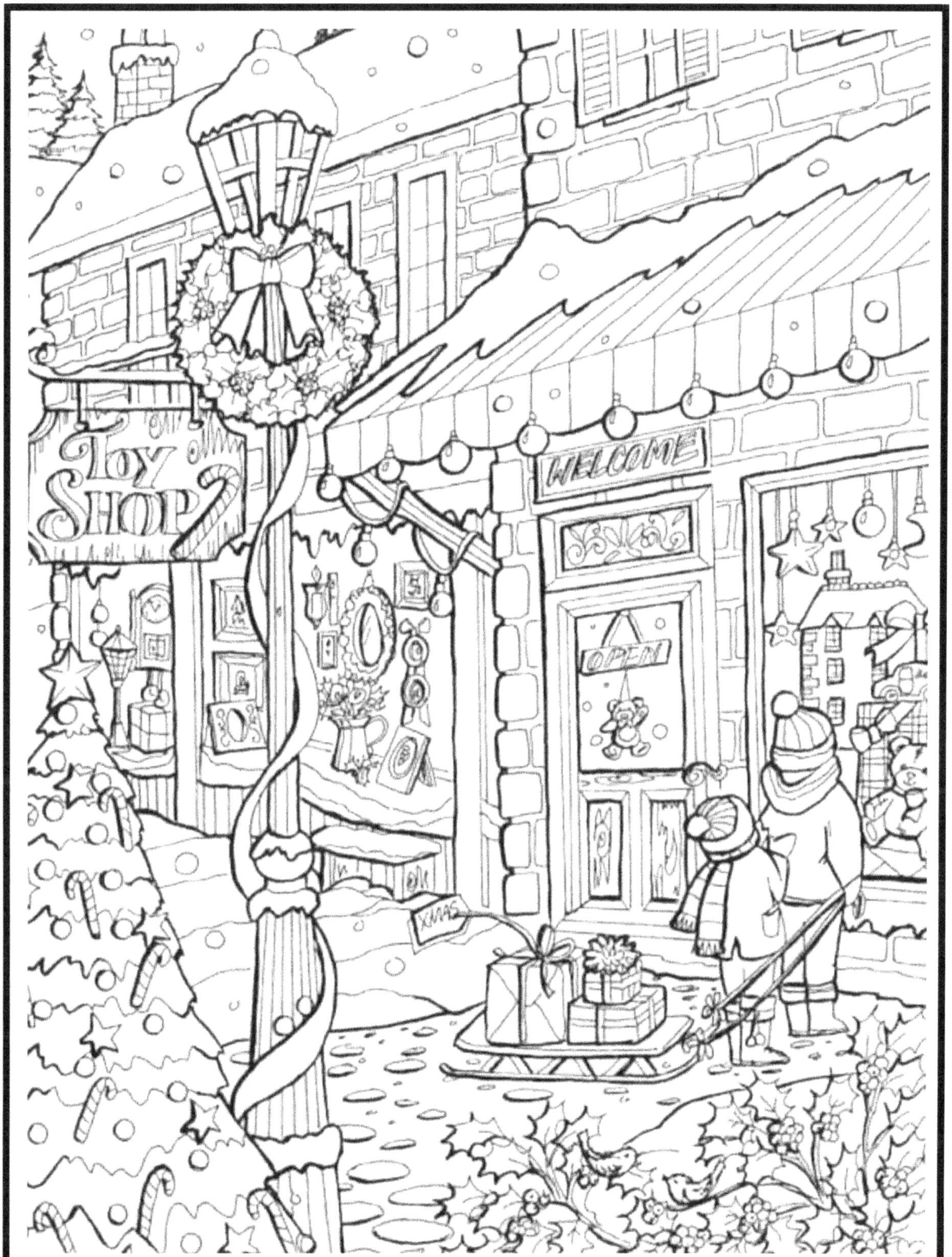
Toy SHOP
WELCOME
OPEN
XMAS

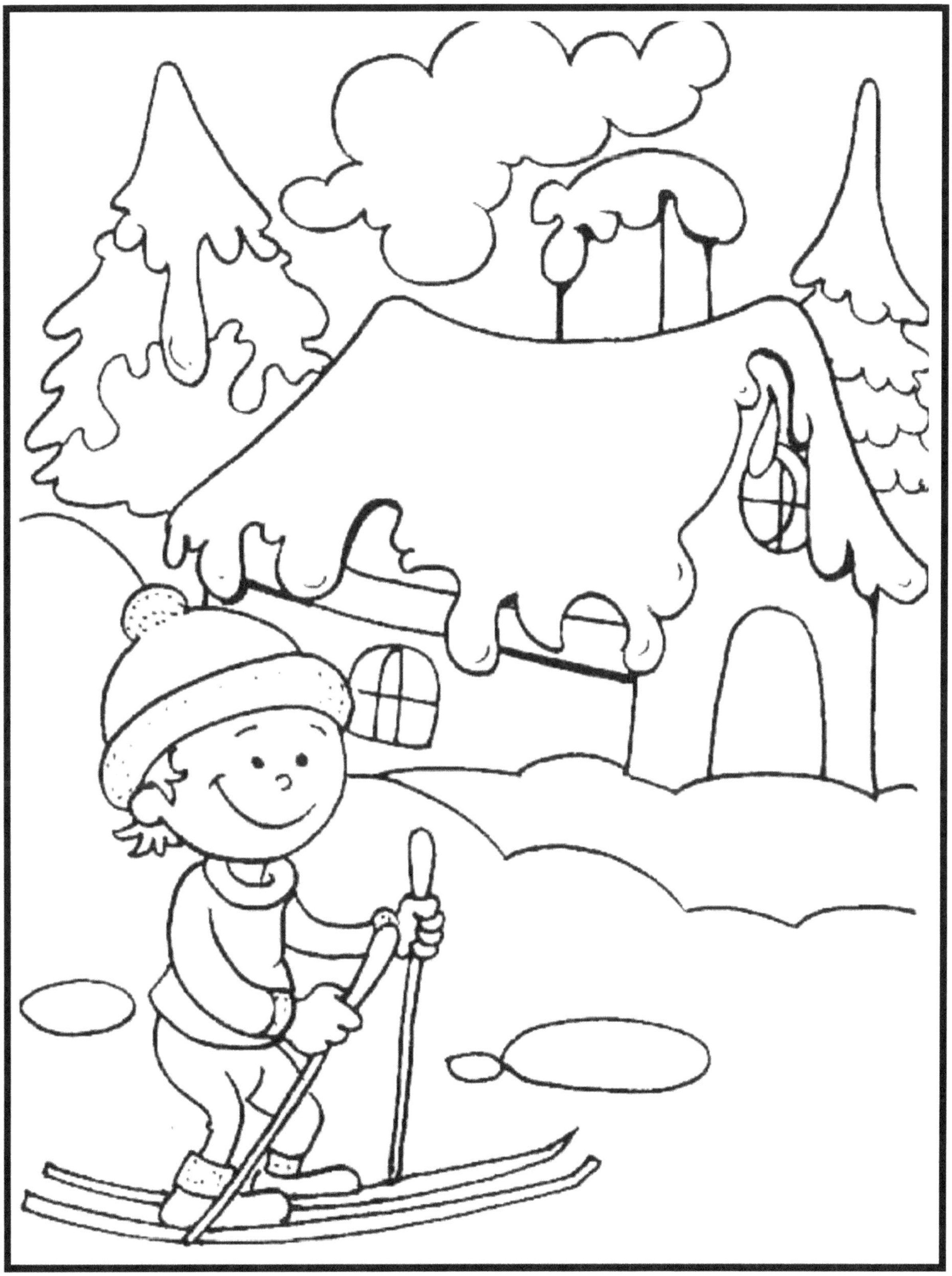

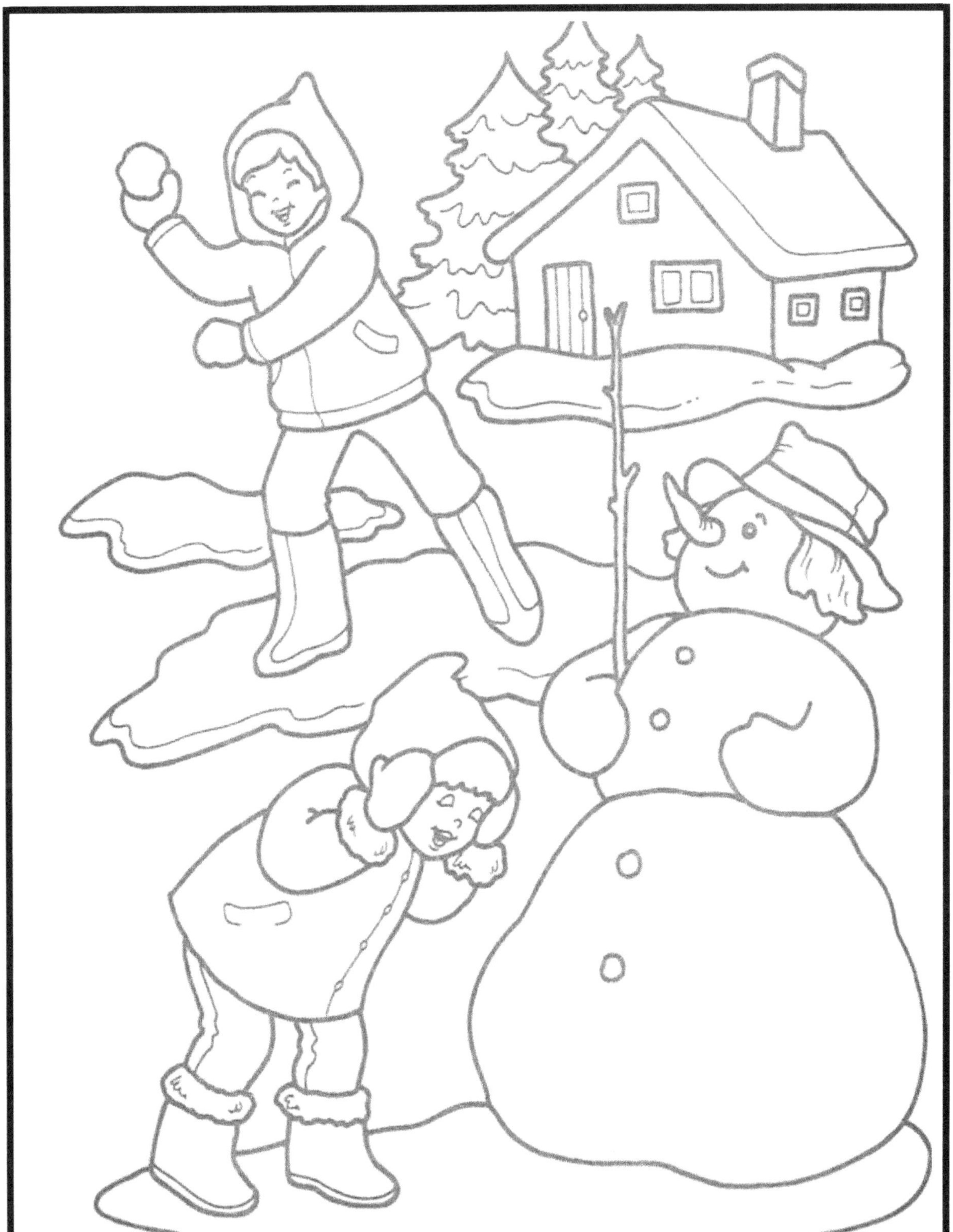

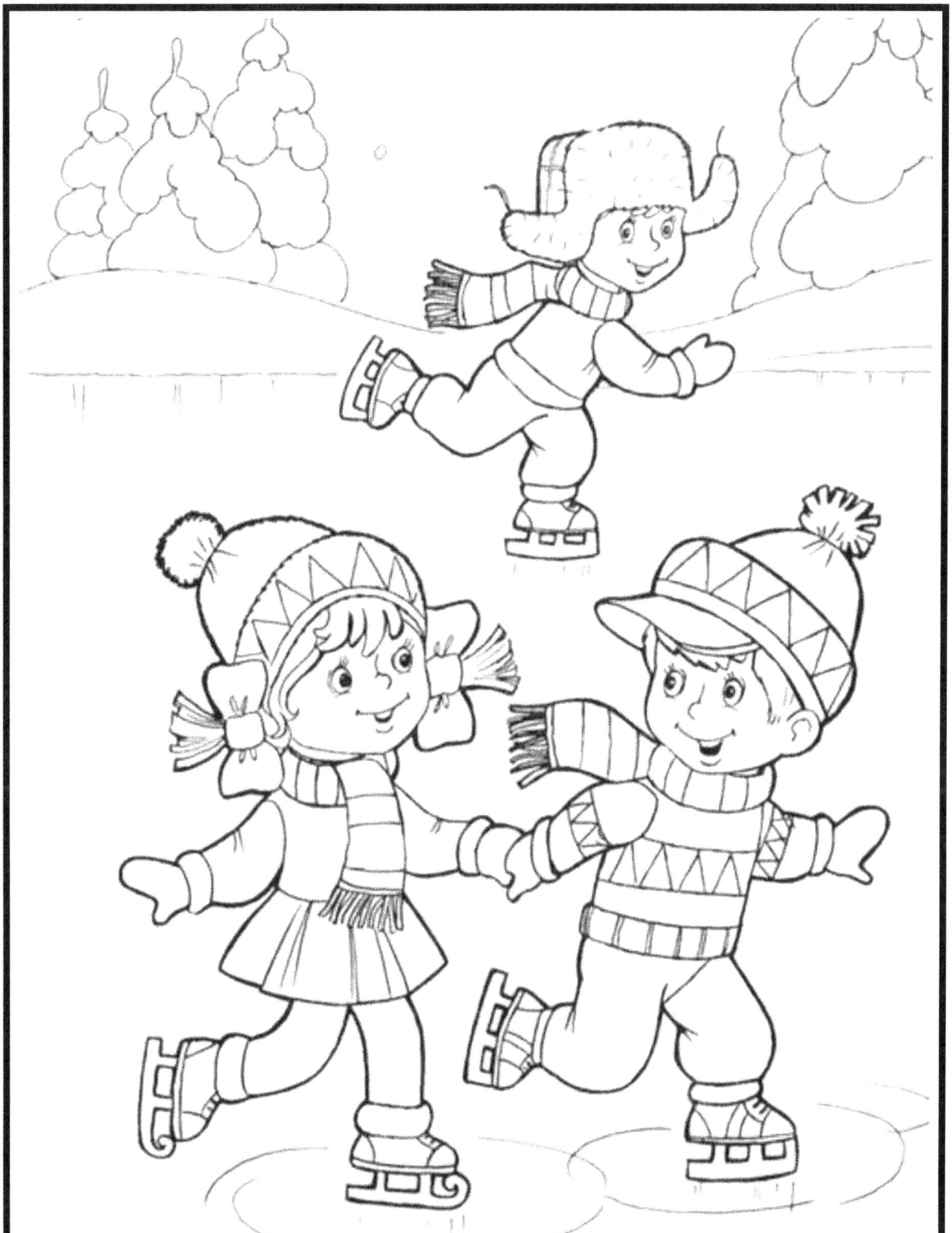

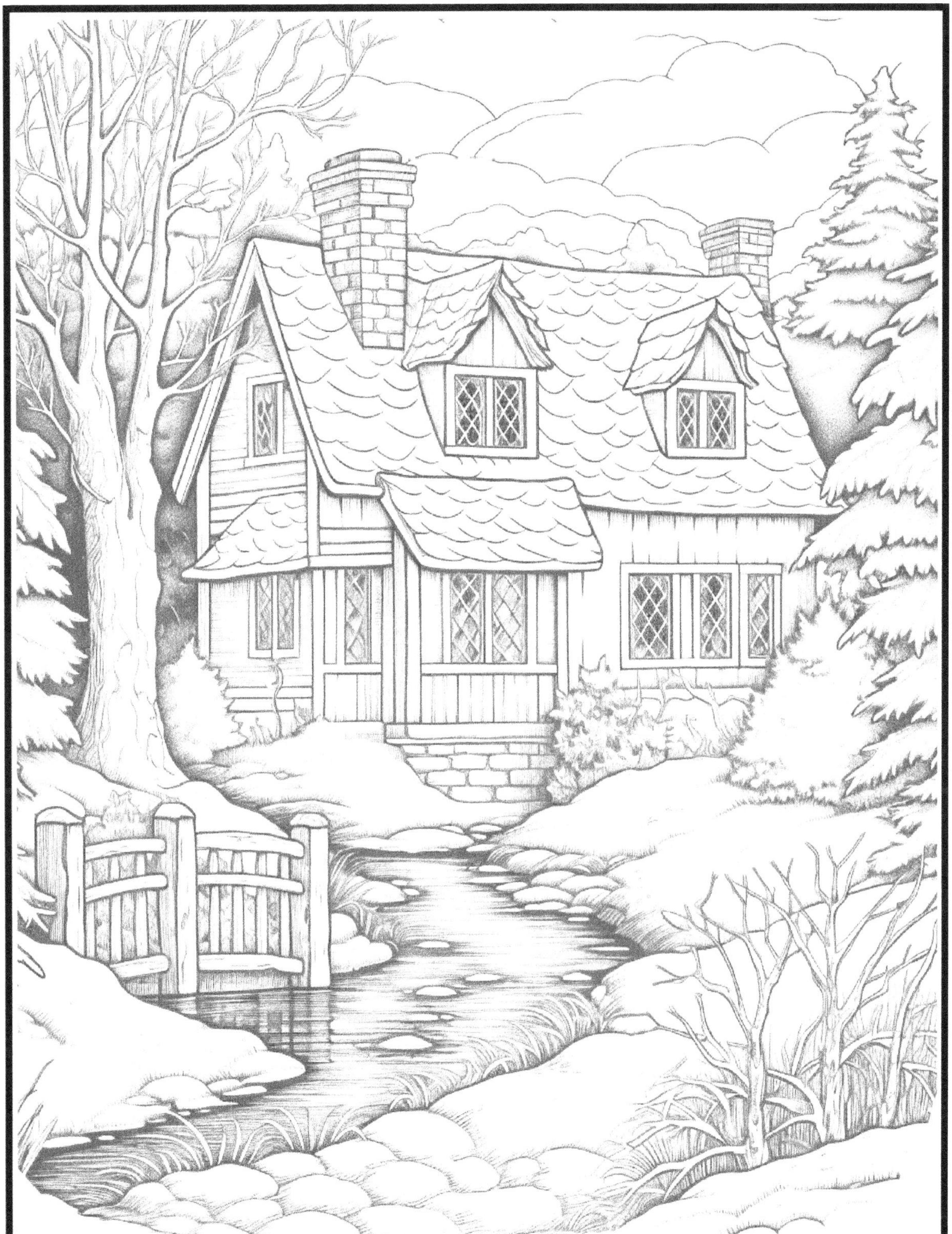

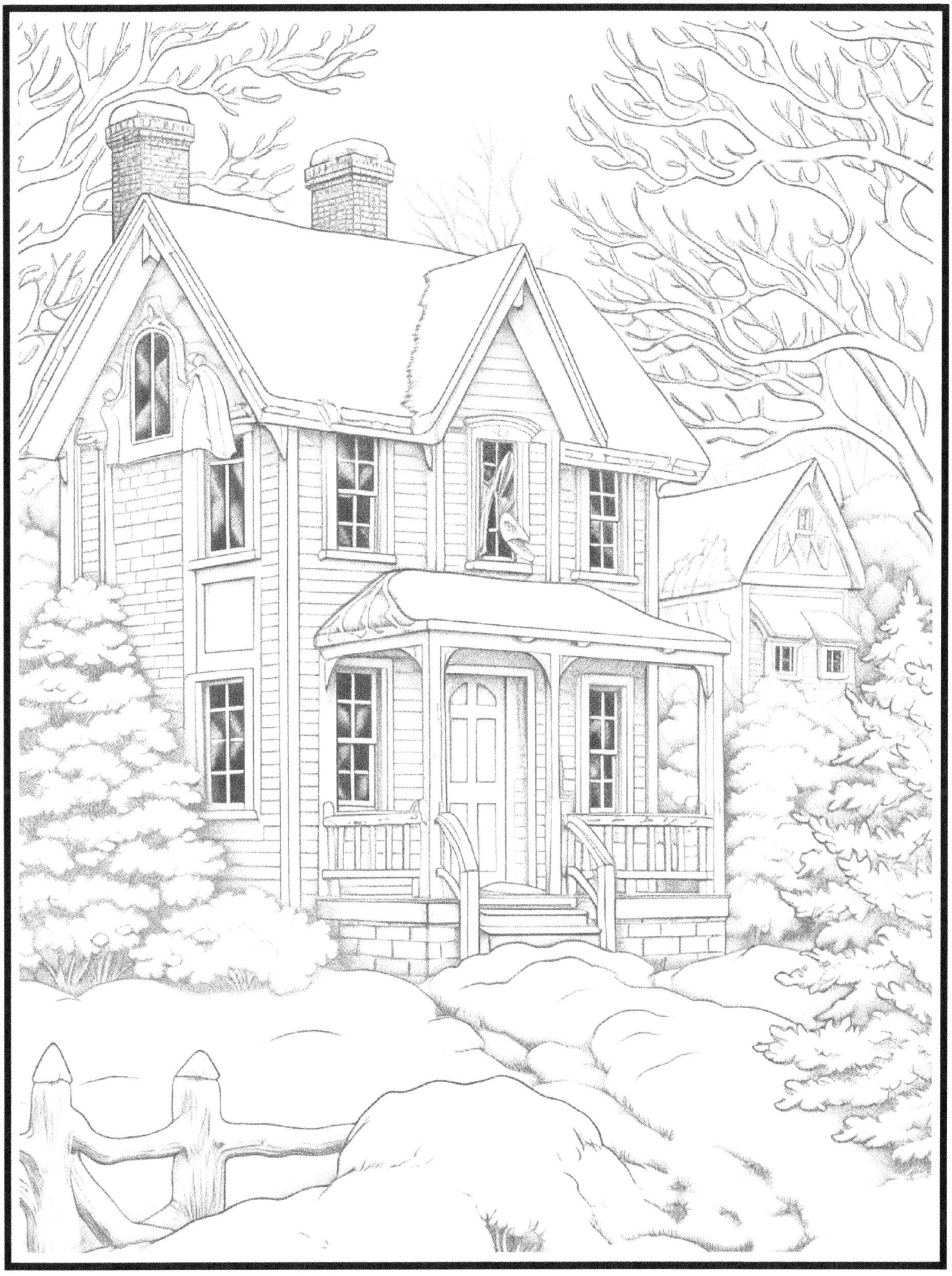

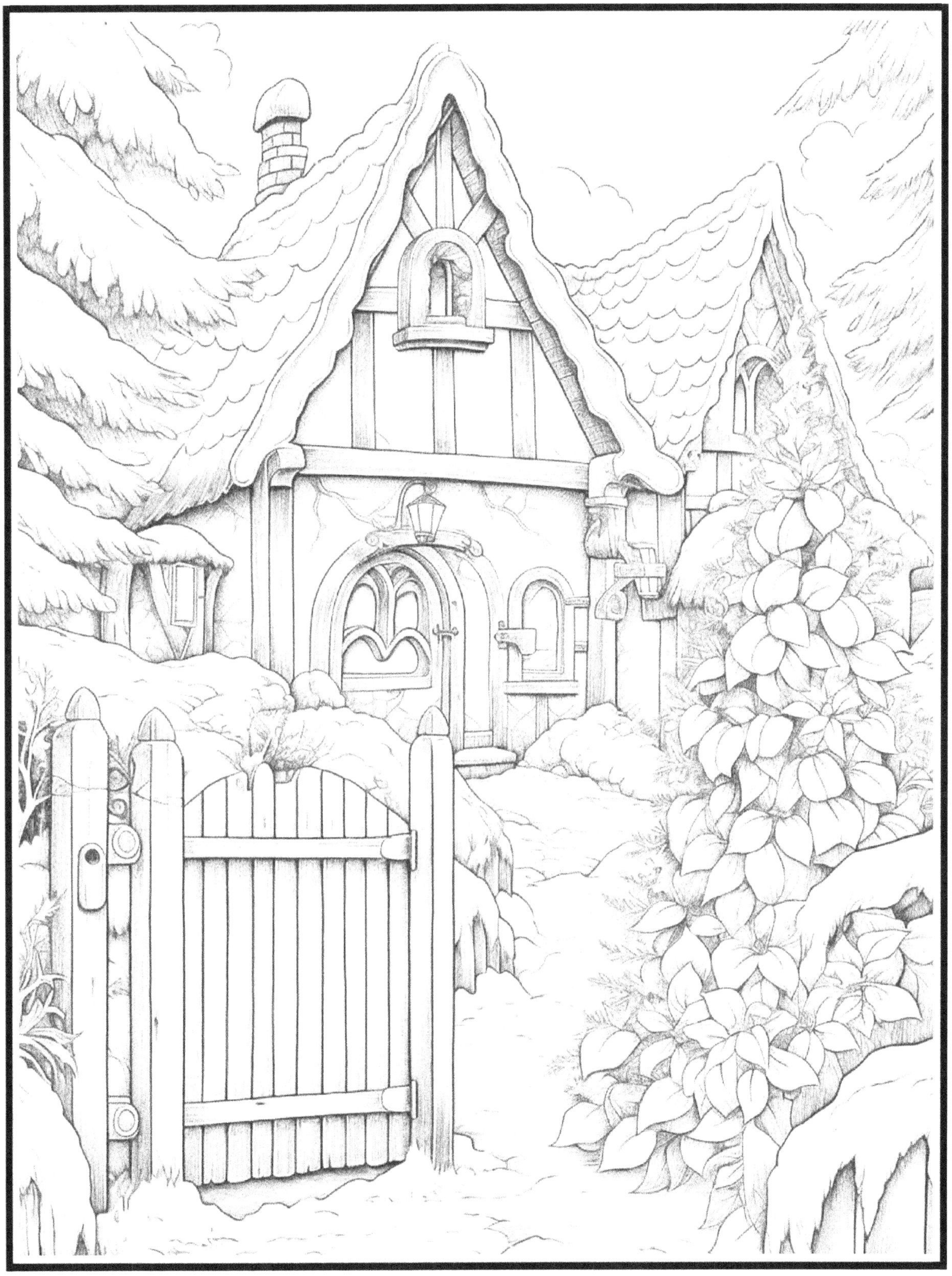

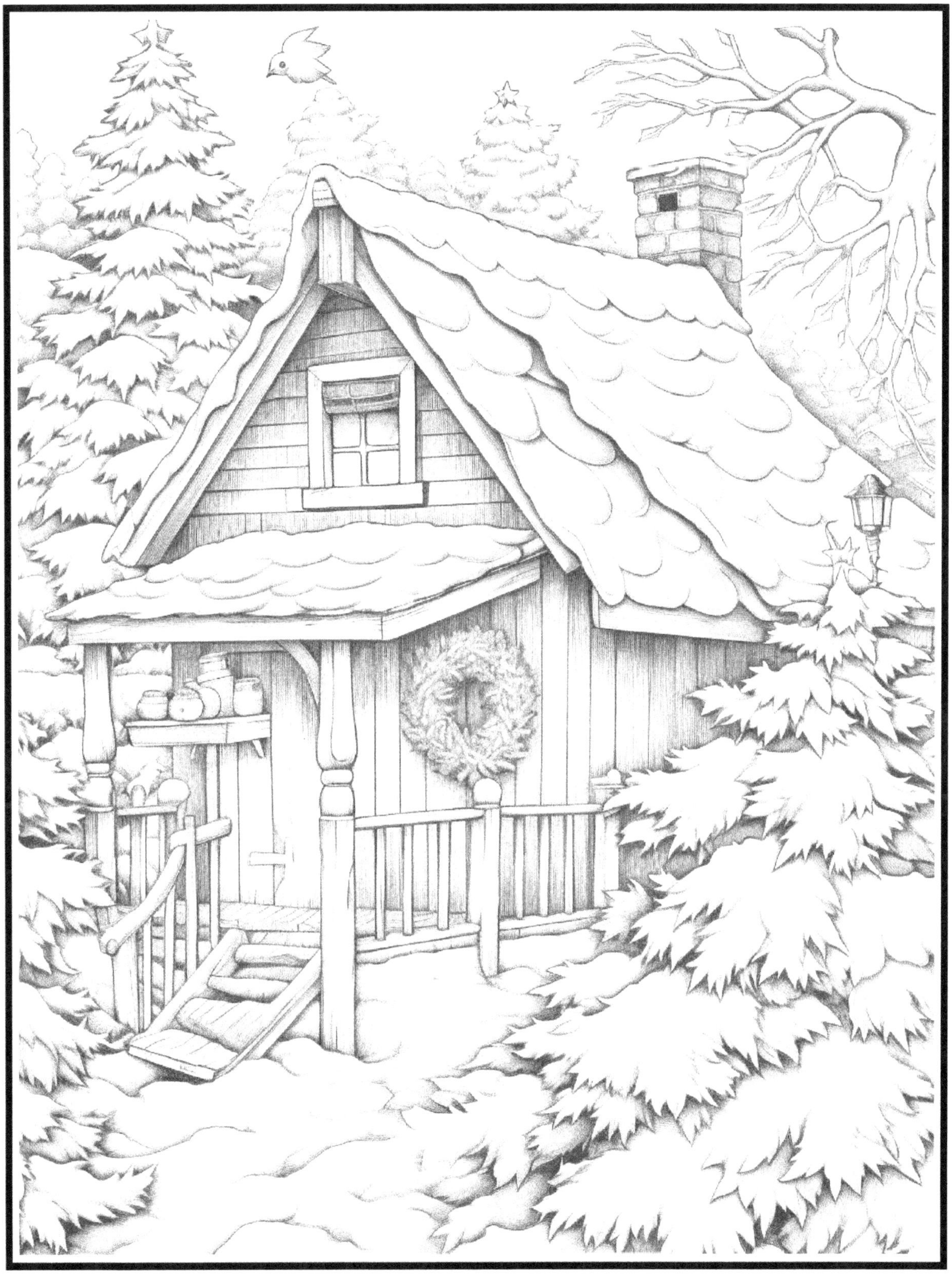

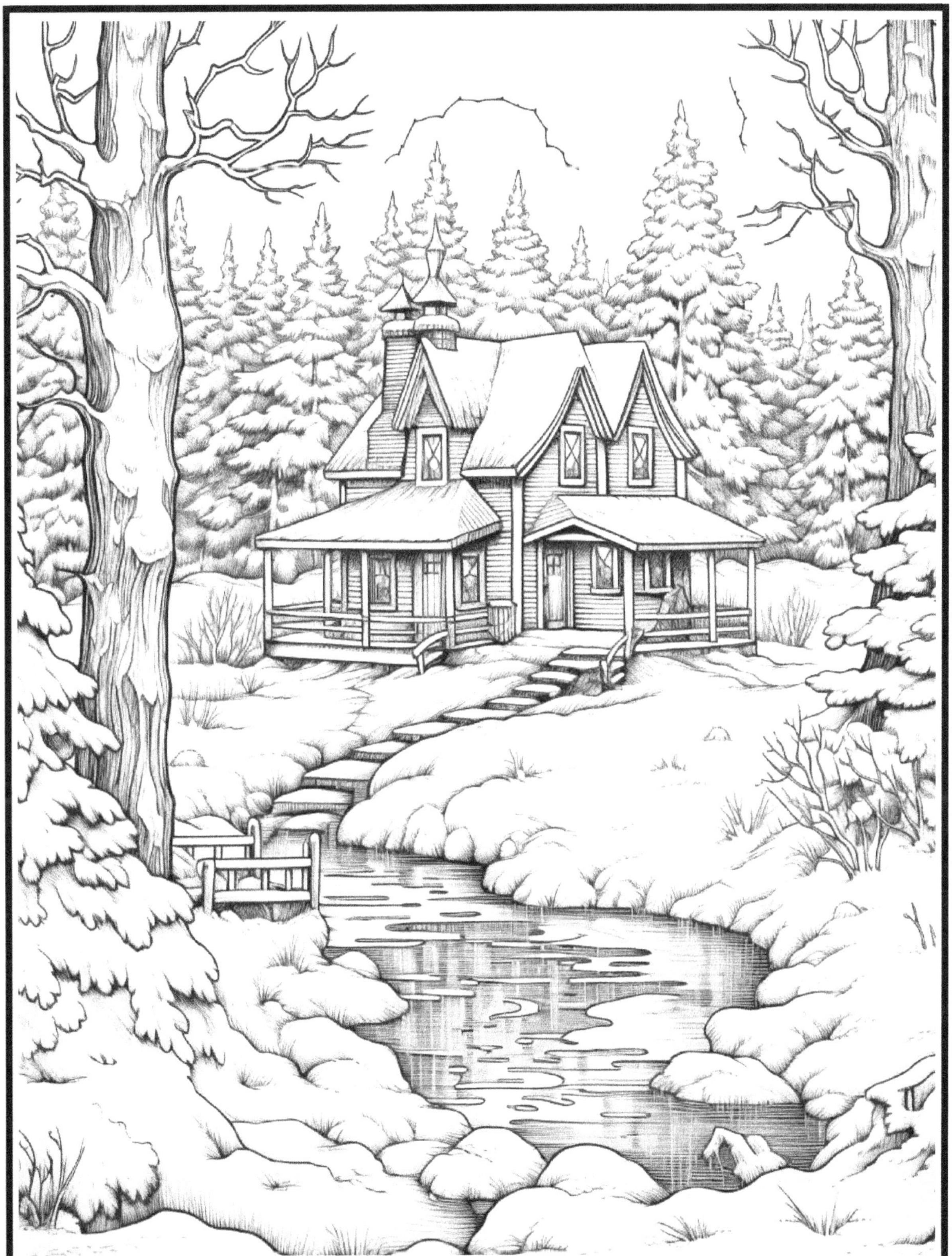

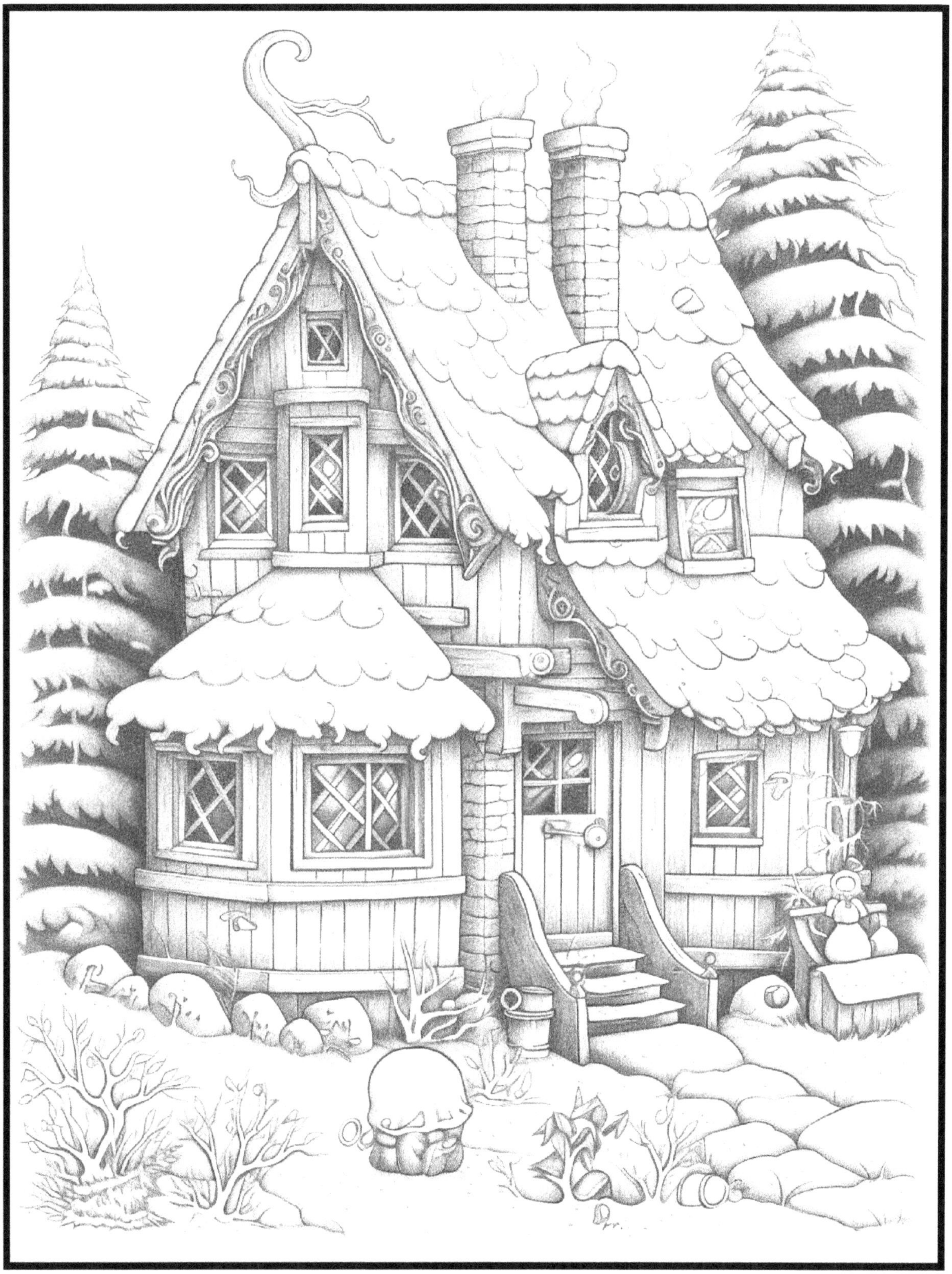

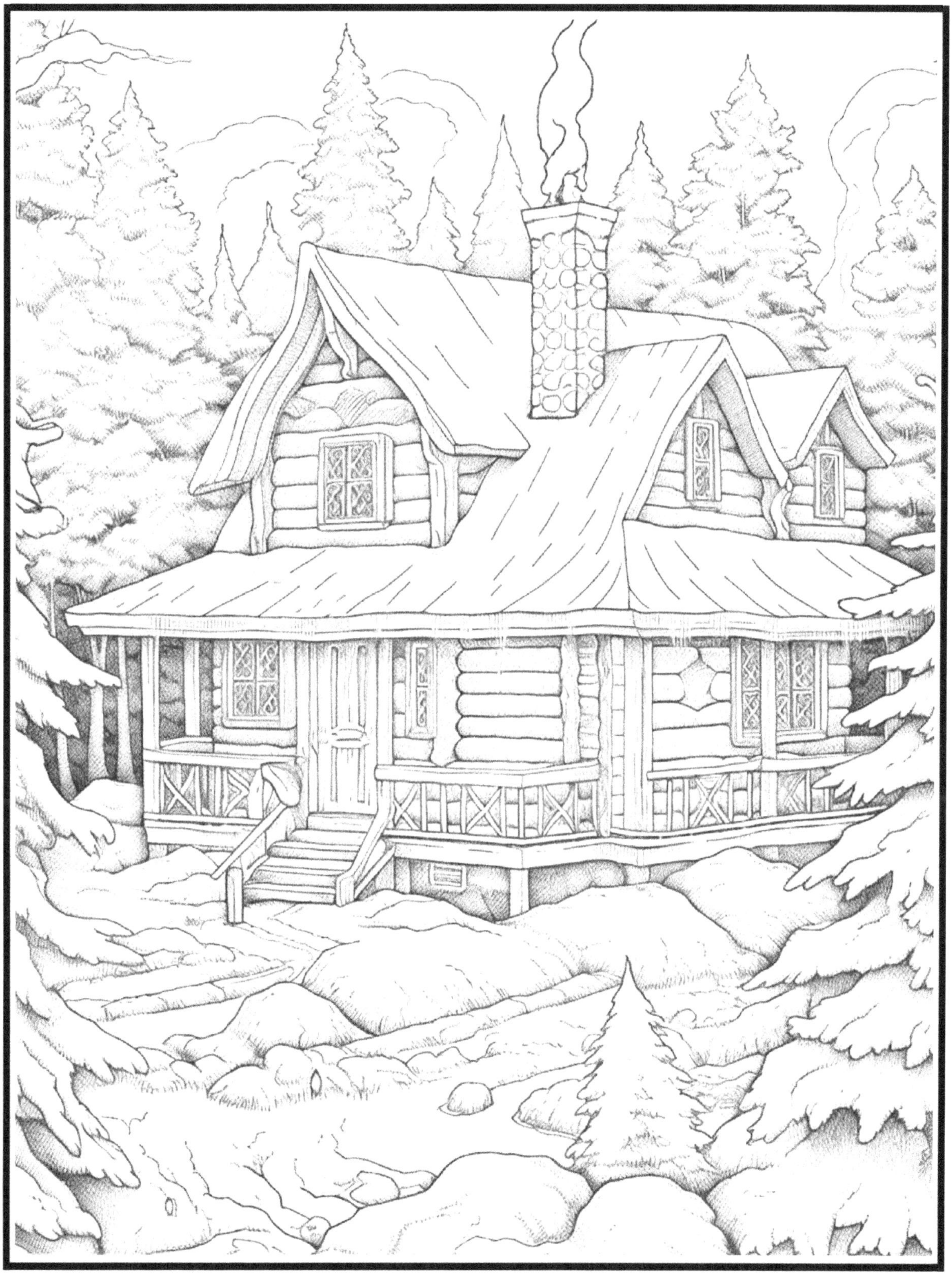

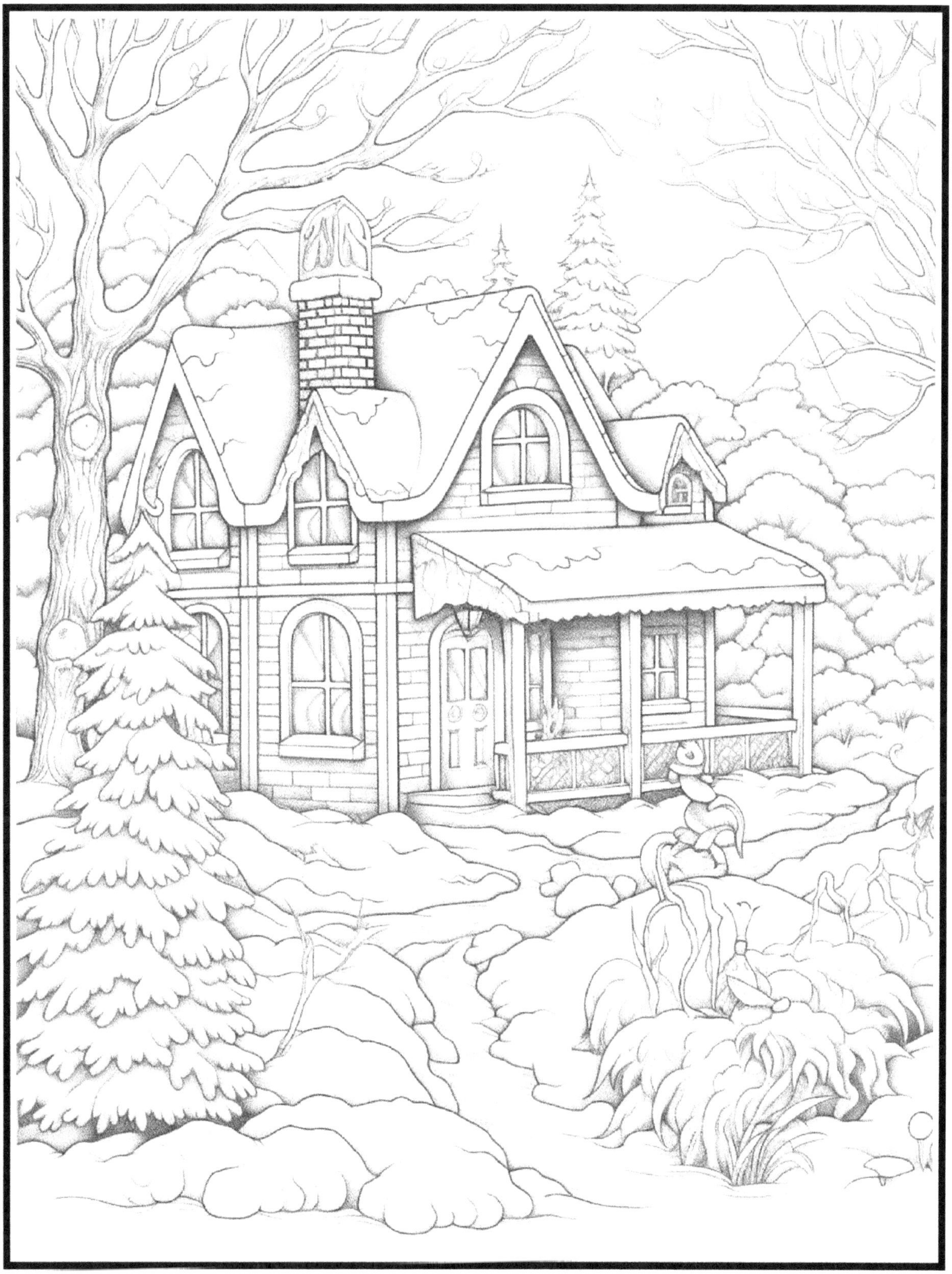

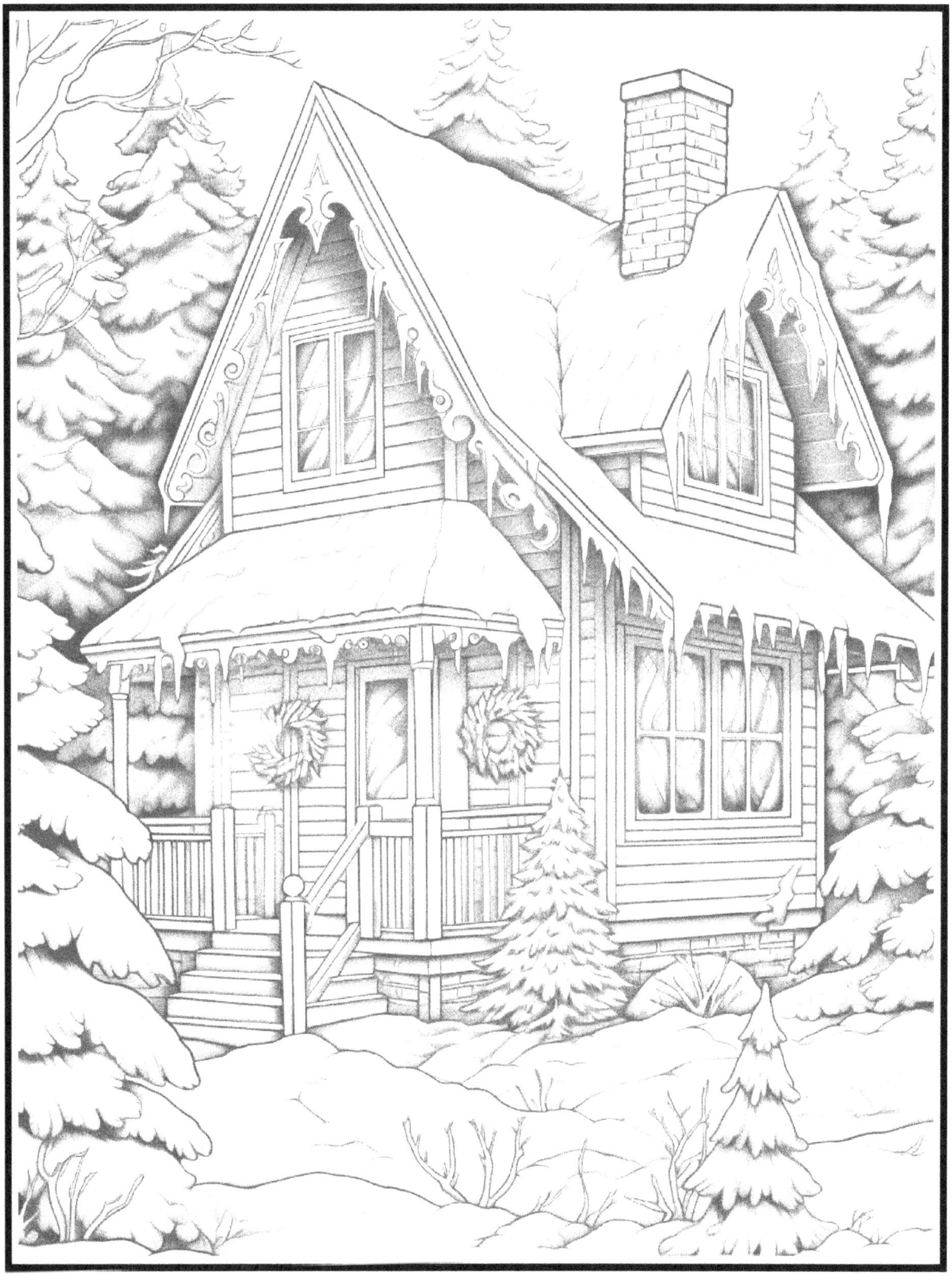

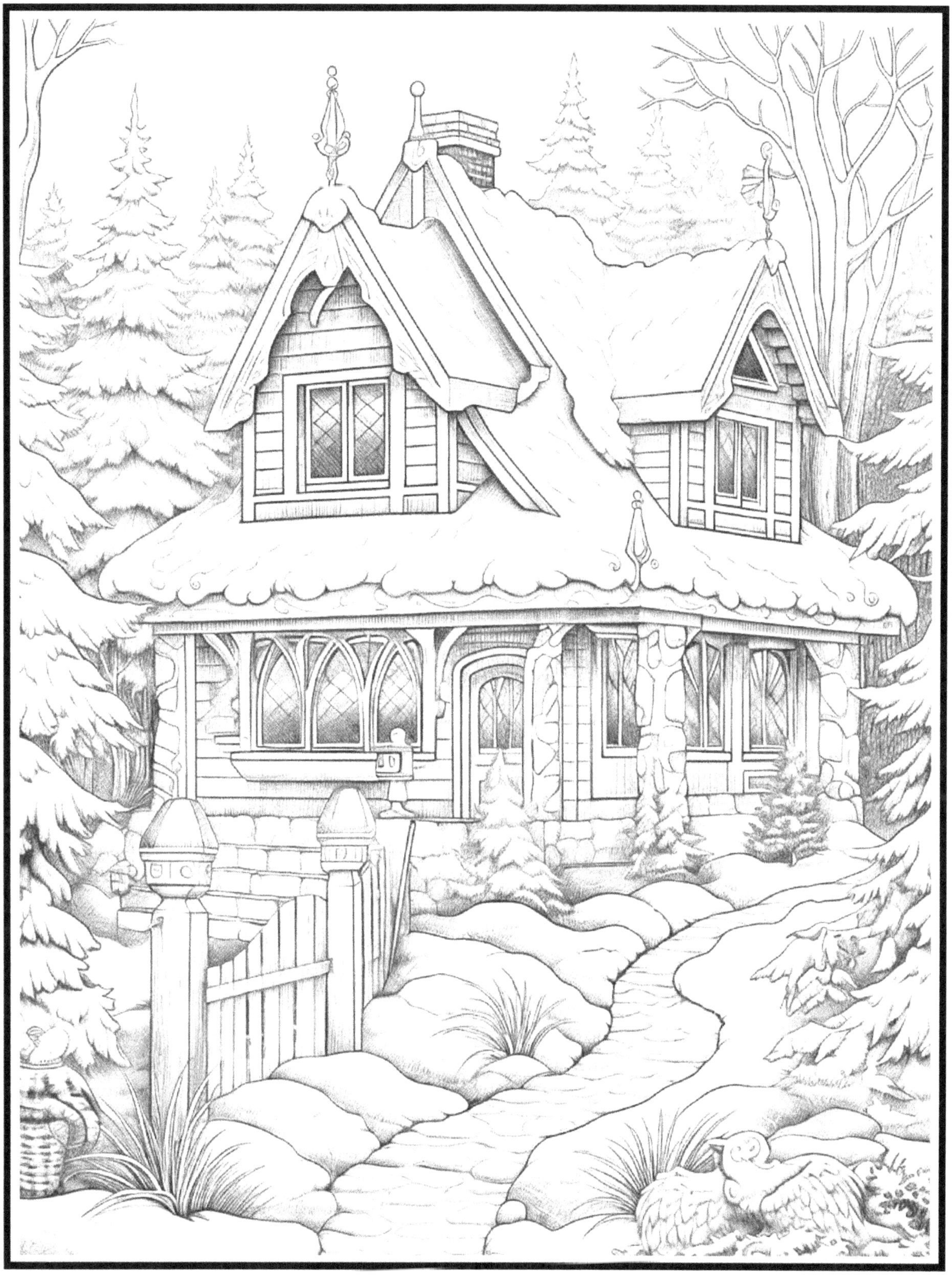

www.ingramcontent.com/pod-product-compliance
Lightning Source LLC
Chambersburg PA
CBHW082220290526
45794CB00009B/3610